# The Wealthy Buddhist

*Rod Burylo*

THE WEALTHY BUDDHIST
Buddhist Ethics, Right Livelihood, and the Value of Money
*Rod Burylo*

Text © Rod Burylo, 2018
All rights reserved

Editing & design by Greenbank Communications
Front & back cover photos by Kapustin Igor, Shutterstock
Author photo by Michelle Burylo

Published by
The Sumeru Press Inc.
402-301 Bayrose Drive, Nepean, ON
Canada K2J 5W3

LIBRARY AND ARCHIVES CANADA CATALOGUING IN PUBLICATION

Burylo, Rod, 1963-, author
    The wealthy Buddhist : Buddhist ethics, right livelihood, and the value of money / Rod Burylo.

ISBN 978-1-896559-41-4 (softcover)

    1. Wealth--Religious aspects--Buddhism. 2. Finance, Personal--Religious aspects--Buddhism. 3. Success in business--Religious aspects--Buddhism. 4. Buddhist ethics. I. Title.

BQ4570.W4B87 2019      294.3'568      C2018-906084-0

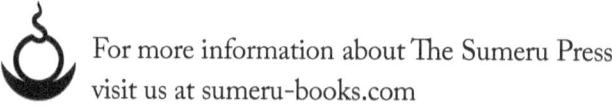

For more information about The Sumeru Press visit us at sumeru-books.com

# Contents

Gratitude ................................... 5

1 A Beginner's Mind ...................... 9

2 Right Livelihood ....................... 21

3 Success and Wealth .................... 33

4 Entrepreneurship and Value Delivery ......... 47

5 Stakeholders and Leaders ................. 63

6 Communication and Trust ................ 79

7 Spending Mindfully .................... 99

8 Investing Mindfully ................... 117

9 Is the Financial Services Industry Trustworthy? 133

10 Impermanence and Opportunity .......... 159

11 A Path Forward ...................... 171

About the Author ......................... 175

# Gratitude

As a person who has enthusiastically pursued ideas, varying perspectives, knowledge, and information, both practical and trivial, I am most fortunate to have ended up in the financial services industry. The opportunities to learn and grow have been constant, and, my life has intersected regularly with the lives of the wonderfully creative and talented. Many have generously mentored and encouraged my progress.

I met David Chilton at a University of Calgary Alumni function. His book, The Wealthy Barber, was extremely popular at that time, and he was busy making the most of his fame. As a successful financial planner myself, I had read the book, though more out of curiosity than out of a desire to gain some new financial wisdom. I was merely interested in reading what my clients were reading, and so I was surprised and endeared by Mr. Chilton's self-deprecating speech regarding his writing abilities and financial education. As I was also working on my own book (another one, not this one), I had an excuse to start a conversation, which I did. Though he offered to be a resource, and provided me with a phone number, I was genuinely surprised when he answered my phone call a few weeks later. He happily shared his thoughts and experiences about writing, publishing, and attracting readers. I had been published as a columnist and contributor to newspapers for a dozen years or so prior to that conversation, and was comfortable with presenting my ideas to the public and receiving constructive criticism. At that time, though, I was suffering from a lack of confidence, and was feeling anxious and vulnerable from the prospect of presenting an entire book to the market. Mr. Chilton gave me the confidence to complete that project: which helped make possible a lifetime of writing and public speaking. Approximately ten years later, Mr. Chilton was a presenter at an educational event in Edmonton. I attended, armed with a copy of my second book, which I offered to him along with my appreciation. As I was preparing to write this particular book – the one that you are now reading – the expression The Wealthy Buddhist kept rising in my consciousness. In being aware of it, and seeking its cause, I couldn't help but to conclude that David Chilton continues to have an impact on my life. Thanks David.

The pursuit of ideas and varying perspectives also led me to the Buddhist community and, in particular, the congregation of The Calgary Buddhist Temple. Not only was I welcomed as a student, I realized that, like me, many of the congregation were seeking wisdom from others. I was quickly invited to contribute what I could to the organization, serving as a Director on the Board for many years, as well as in the capacities of Vice-President and President. This was a challenging and dynamic time for the congregation, as the temple building was deteriorating, and important and difficult decisions were being faced. Ultimately, the congregation and the Board made the brave, and expensive, choice to completely renovate the temple, and re-present it to the City of Calgary with a beautiful, Japanese, Zen-inspired aesthetic. I served as Chair of the capital-raising committee (drawing from experience with finance), which gave me the opportunity to connect with the international community of Buddhists, participating in governance, teaching workshops, and even speaking at a world conference. This experience was transformative for me, as I began to learn about the difference between Buddhism as a collection of historical ideas, or as a mental or intellectual exercise experienced by reading or meditation, and Buddhist ideals as a motivator of, or rationale for, action, enterprise and endeavour in contemporary, Western society. In many ways, this book is about that distinction: between historical Buddhism and modern endeavours: in particular, those regarding the pursuit of wealth. Thanks to The Calgary Buddhist Temple for that experience.

The experiences I have enjoyed have been made ever more sweet and meaningful for having shared these with my loving, and ever patient, wife and partner, Anna. Thank you, Dear.

# 1
# A Beginner's Mind

Do you have specific ideas or feelings about things such as money, wealth, success, and business? Do you ever wonder where these ideas come from? Or perhaps you wonder whether or not these ideas are accurate – do they reflect reality, or are they misguided? Perhaps these perspectives lead to anxiety. Do you worry that the financial acumen and success enjoyed by others will be elusive for you? Perhaps you wonder if those feelings about financial matters are useful. That is, do they help you achieve your financial goals? Or perhaps you wonder if your behaviour concerning how you make, spend and save money is morally appropriate. Perhaps you believe (like some) that being ethical and engaging in business activities are mutually exclusive goals: that those that become rich set aside some of their principles along the way.

These are the sorts of questions that will be explored throughout this book. This exploration will take us into a wide range of topics, including: employment, entrepreneurship, the pursuit of wealth, investments, and the financial services industry. The objective is to not only understand these topics better, but to consider how we might judge our behaviour (as related to these topics) from a moral perspective. In particular, as you might infer from the book's title, this exploration will take us to a destination: the idea that, with the right moral perspective, not only can one achieve wealth in an ethical way, but ethical behaviour can increase the likelihood of being wealthy.

I arrived at this destination in my life after many, many years of education, choices, business ventures, and reflection. The motivation for these pursuits can be traced back to a single event in my life. I cannot explain specifically why I acted the way that I did. Events unfolded quickly, and my behaviour seemed to be completely automatic. I don't recall a single thought as to what the outcome would be, or how others might respond. In that moment, I did not contemplate that I would soon be on the cover of a major print newspaper, a lead story on the televised 6:00 news, and the subject of any family's dinner conversation. Where did my sense of right and wrong, or of duty, or of obligation, come from?

I was not raised with any particular religious belief – at least not in a way that would clearly account for my sense of morality. I was certainly not raised to be Buddhist. My parents were both born in Canada, of families of eastern European descent. My father's parents arrived from Poland and spoke Polish, though it is not at all clear where they were actually from. (I have been told repeatedly that "Burylo" is not a Polish last name). My mother's ancestors also came from Poland, but with more Polish-sounding names. In addition to their language, they brought with them their customs, and their religion. I understand that my father's family went to a Catholic church in Winnipeg, and I have even heard that he was an altar boy. This surprised me. My mother's extended family populated rural Manitoba as farmers, and built what was, in its day, a very large and impressive church. When my father became a member of the Royal Canadian Mounted Police he was posted in British Columbia. It was the custom at the time to have officers posted away from their communities – perhaps away from the influences of friends and family. My mother joined him, also leaving such influences, and the religious community. I was born soon after.

I have only one childhood memory related to a religious activity. I believe I was around five or six years old, when I participated in a presentation of the nativity. This is the story of the birth of the baby Jesus. The presentation featured children of the church congregation in all of the roles: Mary, Joseph, farm animals, etc. I was one of the three wise men who arrived from the East, following the star, and bearing gifts. While I don't remember which particular wise man I was, or the specific gift, I do remember that the gift was represented by a small, empty, glass bowl with a lid. I believe it was a crystal candy dish. I remember this clearly because, as I was waiting with the other little wise men, out of sight of the audience, for our cue to proceed solemnly towards the manger, I dropped the little candy dish and it broke. I remember being quite upset about this, and embarrassed, not only because it was a most inopportune time to break this important prop that had been entrusted to me, but because I thought that it was quite a beautiful little candy dish.

Given the insignificance of organized religion during my childhood, it came as quite a shock to me when I was told at the age of 12 that I would not be proceeding from the local public elementary school to the local high school, with all of my friends. Instead, I was being sent to Notre Dame: a private Catholic school. To add to the disruption, this high school was not in our local community, or even in one of the suburban communities nearby. It was located in a tough, inner-city neighbourhood of the adjacent city of Vancouver. Further, I would need to commute by public transit: a journey that would take an hour or so, each way.

To be clear, though this was technically a private school, it was private in the sense that it was not fully funded by the provincial government (in the way Catholic high schools are funded in other provinces). It was funded, in part, directly by the parents of the students. Thankfully, this was most certainly not a school for the children of wealthy families, for I was not one. (My father was still an RCMP officer, with a steady, though modest, paycheque, and my mom mostly looked after the family home.) As I would quickly come to realize, this Catholic school was centred in the middle of Vancouver's East End. My new classmates were typically of Italian descent. Their parents had come from Europe, as my Grand Parents and Great Grand Parents had, and brought their language (which many still spoke at home), their customs, and their religion.

I was not sent to this school specifically to learn about, and practice Catholicism, although my mother took this turn of events as an opportunity to revisit her own religious inclinations. She initiated a more concerted effort to educate us in her faith, and the associated institution, by adding regular church attendance as a new featured activity of our weekends.

Nor was I sent to this school for the quality of the education it provided: government funds were less that than those provided to public schools, and the working class families of the students had limited financial resources to support additionally. The teaching faculty included a healthy complement of nuns (some of whom lived in a convent attached to the main campus), and the library and science lab were poorly equipped relative to our public school counterparts.

In fact, I was sent to this school to play football. Like its more famous American namesake, this Notre Dame had become quite well-known for fielding exceptional, championship-calibre teams, and produced more than its fair share of professional players. My father was a football fanatic, perhaps even to the point of obsession. Around his policing duties, he found time to coach, referee, organize skills camps, and even serve as the President of the British Columbia Amateur Football Association. My father was as big, tough, and intimidating as you could imagine a cop/football coach would be. Perhaps he expected that 12-year-old-me would get there as well…eventually.

The similarity between the religious experiences and the athletic experience was not lost on me. Pre-game pep rallies gave license for a vocalization of spirit almost evangelical in nature. Coaches and assistants would enter, like an Archbishop with clerics, and star athletes were held in canonical reverence. The congregation prayed in unison for victory.

By my assessment, having me learn to play football was likely intended to be pragmatic. If I were to excel at this sport (as my father hoped that I would), then perhaps this would assist in being admitted to university, provide some much needed financial support (in the form of scholarships), and pave the way to completing a post-secondary education. The objective, I assume, was that this would help me realize a degree of success and wealth that my parents had not. This was a reasonable, middle class dream.

However, I did not grow to become big enough to excel at football (or any other scholarship-worthy sport), even if my heart was in it, which it was not. True to the cliché, the lack of enthusiasm for my father's beloved sport disappointed him greatly.

Meanwhile, my interest in Catholicism was not faring any better. I was being properly introduced to the related ideas, the stories and the history, and to the ritual and practices. I found much of what I was learning to be very puzzling, and though I was coming to understand the perspective of the faithful, I was not becoming one myself. Despite this, I was accepted by the community and participated enthusiastically. I simply kept some of my more controversial philosophical meanderings to myself.

It was with this specific high school experience that I would find myself soon after graduation, struggling as a university student, and the subject of an unlikely event that would set the course of much of my life.

I did manage to get accepted to a local university, though just barely. It was there, upon entering my first actual science lab, that I realized how poorly prepared I was for the experience. While freshman with public school educations quickly set about busying themselves with a comfort born of familiarity, I floundered. My grades reflected that fact, and I became concerned that I would not be permitted to continue with my education.

To make matters worse, I did not seem to have the time available that would be required to improve my academic performance. Without athletic scholarships covering costs, and coming from a family of meagre financial means, I spent that time working. It took many, many hours of employment, at minimum wage, just to cover the costs of tuition, books, and some social life. It was the first time

## The Wealthy Buddhist

I recall really recognizing a true benefit of wealth, and wishing I had access to it.

One of the first jobs I landed was working at a small, local convenience store. This included cleaning, stocking shelves, and manning one of only two cash registers. Lottery tickets were a popular draw for clientele, and the scratch-and-win version had recently been introduced. Prior to these, gamblers had to wait to learn of the outcome. The new lottery tickets offered happiness or disappointment with immediacy.

One day, while I was working, a man came into the store to purchase a $1 ticket. As it wasn't particularly busy, he stood at the counter and started to scratch the six boxes, to see if a prize would be revealed. He scratched them purposefully: the first box, then the second, then the third, the fourth, the fifth…and then he stopped. I would soon see what he saw: that in two of the first five boxes a possible award of $50.00 was indicated. However, he would have to have another $50 indicated in the final box to earn that prize. He started to scratch the sixth box, but just enough to see if the number "5" would be revealed. To his disappointment, the number revealed began with a "1", and so he stopped scratching and left the ticket on the counter. He walked out of the store.

My co-worker next to me, picked up the ticket and started to scratch the rest of that sixth box, as I moved in closer for a look myself. Instantly, her face went white, and it seemed as she would faint. I reached out to catch her and the ticket, and quickly realized the cause of her emotional state. The sixth box, now fully scratched, revealed that the number "1" continued, and was part of the number "10,000". In fact, two of the other five boxes also showed "10,000" as the potential prize – which was apparently missed by the purchaser of the ticket. This ticket was indeed a $10,000 instant-win ticket – the greatest prize available on those tickets at the time!

I sometimes try to imagine what might have gone through my mind at that moment, as I held that ticket. Perhaps I would first have thought about purchasing a car. I suspect that, soon after, my practical side would have also had a say in how best to enjoy that fortune: pay for school! Though $10,000 may not seem like much today, at that time, it would have pretty much covered the entire cost of an under-graduate degree. Such winnings would have a very significant impact on my life: allowing me to stop working, so that I could focus entirely on school, and increase the likelihood of passing my courses. I wonder what I might have thought…had I paused to think…but I did not.

From somewhere inside me, a form of instinct kicked in. I moved without forethought, frantically, out of the store, to the parking lot, looking for the person who had purchased the ticket. I saw him in his car, about to pull out of the stall. I ran to his window and signalling him to roll it down. "Hey mister, you just won $10,000!" He stared at me with a look of disbelief and minor shock, and I actually assisted in putting the car, which had continued to move, back in to Park.

Having gained his composure, and a potentially life-changing lottery ticket, the man went on his way, and I returned to the store. It was then that the full implication of the day's event presented itself. I had a $10,000 winning ticket in my hand and gave it away. It seemed surreal. Why had I done that?

This might have been a question that I would consider privately, but as this happened not long before Christmas, the day's event was becoming a story, and the story was being shared. Newspaper reporters began to call the store, then TV reporters and cameras showed up. We became a lead story on the front page of a major Greater Vancouver newspaper, and a feature on the televised, evening news.

It is hard to say how many people learned about my behaviour over the days that followed. Hundreds of thousands? Over a million? Certainly it seemed a great number of them had an opinion about its appropriateness. Friends and family telephoned to discuss the news, and share their thoughts, to both myself and my parents. Store customers, and complete strangers, came into the store to see the two clerks, and offer their assessment. As you might guess, many of the comments were very positive: I was informed that I had done the right thing, and I was described as honest and generous. However, and to my surprise, many comments were not positive; I was told that I had made the wrong choice of behaviour, and was told that I was foolish and stupid. Perhaps the most disappointing and unsettling feedback came from my father, who told me that if I were to ever to do something like that again I should not bother to come home. I am not sure exactly how serious that comment was meant to be, but I took it to heart.

With all the attention and feedback, I was drawn into discussion. With increasing anxiety, I felt obliged to provide an explanation for my behaviour. I knew that I had not made a specific, conscious decision resulting from some process of reason or argument, to act as I did. I could not find any particular set of learned values or principles that would have wired me for this response to this circumstance. To those who criticized my behaviour, I felt particularly obliged to offer some rationale and justification. I wanted to believe that I had performed the morally correct action. I certainly wanted my father to believe that as well. Yet, I could not find a satisfactory defence for my behaviour in any of the most obvious places: not my family history and culture, not my socioeconomic conditions, not my education, not even religion (as it had been presented to me).

Moreover, I wanted to believe that I had behaved appropriately from a financial perspective. I wanted to understand that my choice of action was more than "morally correct, but stupid." I wanted to believe, and hoped that others might believe, that somehow this behaviour was both ethical and financially appropriate – as far-fetched as that may sound to some.

It was from this desire to defend my action that I was set on a life-long path of education, information gathering, and contemplation. Two themes have been interwoven with this pursuit: money and morality.

With a beginner's mind, I switched from a study of sciences to a study of philosophy. My grades improved dramatically, as I found that my natural propensities were well suited to this new discipline. I was introduced to a very wide range of topics, including Buddhism, but my focus became the study of ethics and jurisprudence, and I had a particular interest in business ethics. Despite my growing academic success and enthusiasm, declaring Philosophy as my major only served to confuse my father and contribute to his general sense of dismay. Nevertheless, my confidence grew considerably during the last few years of university, and I graduated determined to parlay my education into success and financial wealth.

The financial services industry provides a vast opportunity for continuing education, and I have been hungrily consuming that education throughout my career. As I gained experience in each major sector (banking, insurance, investments, financial planning), I completed the associated courses and programs, and earned designations along the way: including Certified Financial Planner, Chartered Investment Manager, and Fellow of the Canadian Securities Institute. With study, and lots of hard work, I began to generate success; my income grew, and accolades were earned – including being a recipient of a prestigious Advisor of the Year Award.

Perhaps I shouldn't complain about an industry that provided me with the means to support my family and enjoy an above average quality of life, but I have been frequently disappointed – even embarrassed – by the prevalence of low moral standards. I have worked hard to try to improve some of the unsavoury aspects of this business: providing ethics audits of financial advisors, drafting codes of ethics and values statements, even creating entire new companies with a focus on improving processes. My skills and experience as a philosopher, and specifically as an ethicist, have provided me with some unexpected advantages in this regard. As a columnist, contributor and media source for more than thirty years, and as an international speaker, I have made a conscious effort to bring the perspectives and the approach of a philosopher to my communications. As you might imagine, such an approach would not be common among my colleagues. Differentiation, however, can create advantages, and I have been able to have my voice heard (in a very noisy industry): as a keynote presenter at client events, as a teacher of ethics classes for financial advisors, as a Chief Compliance Officer, and as Director of public and private companies.

Ironically, this interest in business and ethics, and the willingness to act in an attempt to improve, has made the biggest difference in my personal wealth creation objectives. While my work as a financial advisor produced a good living, and the experience and education I gained is certainly helpful in understanding how to manage wealth when it is received, it was only by pursuing problem-solving business opportunities that I have created financial independence.

In this book, I will discuss this form of wealth creation, and how the pursuit of wealth can be aided by a strong sense of morality. I have learned that there are specific approaches and perspectives that can dramatically increase the likelihood of achieving success. Indeed, I will argue that the pursuit of wealth can be more than merely aided by a strong moral compass: that this pursuit can be a moral obligation. This obligation also has implications for how we spend, save and invest our money, as well as how we engage with others in a work environment. These topics will be addressed in detail, in the hopes that you not only gain some practical information that may guide your decision-making as it relates to the money that you make, but that you receive some inspiration to strive to make ethical choices along the way.

As the financial services industry often presents itself as the provider of wealth creation and maintenance solutions, I will also address (and challenge) the relevance of this industry to your financial pursuits. I will offer a critique both about the value that many industry participants propose to provide to consumers, as well as my concerns about corporate culture, values, ethics, and trustworthiness.

## A Beginner's Mind

This intellectual journey that we will embark upon together has a starting point. It begins with a specific philosophical tradition: Buddhism. More than any other collection of ideas, observations and prescriptions, those of Buddhism have proved to be most useful to me as I have grappled with so many ethical questions and moral dilemmas, especially as they relate to making, spending and saving money. Moreover, these ideas have figured prominently in my successes as an employee, as a professional, as a manager, as an executive, and most especially as an entrepreneur.

If I have any regret about the education and wisdom I have received since the incident concerning the lottery ticket, it is that it came too slowly. It has only been relatively recently that I have been able to make sense of my choice that day, and been quite comfortable in defending it. Sadly, I never did have the opportunity to present this case to my father, nor demonstrate to him my abilities to achieve financial success. He died suddenly and much too young, just when my career was beginning to show signs of promise. This effort, then, that I make over the coming pages, is not motivated by being a son, but motivated by being a father.

My own children came when I was young and still in university, and I have welcomed the opportunity to parent, and guide, and mentor, as they have grown. The message of this book, to them, and to you, is first to seek understanding with an open mind – a beginner's mind. Seek perspectives and ideas beyond those that are presented to you by your family, your community, or your religion. This is especially true when it comes to learning about making money and creating wealth. A great many ideas about business, investing and wealth are imparted by parents, teachers, and others, who, though well-meaning, have not themselves achieved a level of success that would assure expertise of these subjects. Rather, wealth is more likely to result from seeking, and being open to, new sources of information, ideas, and perspectives – hopefully, like those presented over the coming pages.

# 2
# Right Livelihood

Philosophy is a discipline that challenges the student to question what they think they know. It asks that they be prepared to question those ideas which they hold most closely. In the process, we sometimes come to realize that some of our ideas about what is true or not, or what we think we should do or not do, must be abandoned. I think of philosophical efforts as being about more than the pursuit of knowledge, but about being the pursuit of useful ideas. This helps me to judge the success of these efforts. While whether or not a particular idea or statement can be determined true may be important in some instances, I am often more intrigued by the question of whether or not an idea is useful. I ask: does this idea help me make better choices that will produce the outcomes I am striving for?

An effort to understand the basic ideas of Buddhism, for example, may produce this result.

Buddhist thought covers a vast array of topics, ideas and statements. It comprises a repository of material contributed by a wide range of philosophers and students over a very long period of time. It has been said that, as this intellectual tradition was introduced to new cultures by the teachers who travelled, the expression of Buddhism in thought and practice would change: each, the philosophy and the culture, being altered by the process. Buddhism is typically described as being one of the world's great religions, but it is significantly different in at least one, most important way: the intellectual tradition I associate with Buddhism does not begin with the postulation of the existence of a deity.

## The Wealthy Buddhist

To be clear, in my many years of study, and active involvement in the Western Buddhist community, I have also never heard it postulated that there is not a deity. A belief in the possibility of the existence of God, or a god, seems to me to be not inconsistent with the core of Buddhist thought, even if it is not explicitly discussed. This (relative) silence on the matter of deism is a very critical point when it comes to an understanding of a Buddhist approach to morality and money. For, if a requirement for the existence of a god or God is not the premise on which a meaningful moral philosophy is based, what is that premise?

The entirety of a Buddhist thought is, in fact, associated with a specific idea. I believe that many, when they first begin to learn about this religion, are surprised at what that idea is. The surprise may come from their expectation about what a philosophy must have or be to become considered a religion. Or the surprise may come from an association of Buddhism with a statue, and making assumptions about what that statue represents. These assumptions may be the result of our perspectives about religion in general, or about the religion of our upbringing. Regardless, many are surprised to learn that Buddhism can feel quite different from other religions.

Buddhism begins with a relatively simple idea: that people are often unhappy. In some cases this unhappiness might be described as mild irritation, or being really pissed off, or being in a full-blown state of suffering. Further, it is proposed that this state of unhappiness is associated with needs, wants, and desires. In fact, Buddhism clarifies this association by postulating that the relationship between wants and unhappiness is causal; that is, if one can reduce or eliminate the wanting, then the unhappiness can be reduced or eliminated, resulting in increased happiness. The final concept associated with this foundational understanding of the state of things: indeed, you can, I can, and we can reduce or eliminate the unhappiness. These ideas are typically referred to as the Four Noble Truths.

## Right Livelihood

When I was first introduced to this idea, I had difficulty in understanding it, and made a mistake in my reasoning. I understood that it was being proposed that when there is unhappiness, there is want, and when there is want, there is unhappiness. I misunderstood that it was being proposed that want is both a necessary and sufficient condition for the existence of unhappiness. This did not sit well with me, as I considered the possibility that I would want to help another person, and this want could lead to action, which would result in the other person being helped, and more happiness created. Buddhism does not propose that wanting necessarily leads to unhappiness, but that, when there is unhappiness, there is want.

To clarify this, consider the relationship between an egg and an omelette. If there is an omelette, there were eggs, because (by definition) an omelette is comprised of eggs. However, the presence of eggs (want) does not necessarily mean that the presence of an omelette (increased unhappiness) will result. Instead, other things might result: such as a cake, or French toast, or an egg salad sandwich, or a baby bird. If there is an omelette, there were eggs, but if there are eggs, with guidance, a baby chick could result instead.

It is important to note that this premise for Buddhism is arrived at through experience. It is not the case that one is invited to accept the idea of the existence of unhappiness or suffering based upon faith. One is invited to observe their own instances of unhappiness, and try to determine if there is some form of want or desire that may be the cause. I have been conducting my own self-observation for many years, and have found that when I have feelings of unhappiness, or even the occasional feelings of anger, I can see that specific wants are present.

How we might set about accomplishing the objective of reducing want and increasing happiness is really the value proposition of Buddhism, and much of the philosophy and practice is about this pursuit. The word most used to describe this value proposition is dharma, or teachings. Within the dharma, the most commonly discussed collection of ideas on how one can reduce want and increase happiness is referred to as the Eight-Fold Path. This path expresses eight distinct, though inter-related, concepts and behavioural prescriptions.

The eight concepts are thought to be categorized into three groups: Wisdom, Ethical Conduct, and Mental Discipline.

These ideas, when presented verbally or in writing, are described in a particular order. However, these ideas are also very often presented visually, and, in this case, are represented by a circle with eight lines radiating from the centre, symmetrically, in eight directions. It is like a wheel with eight spokes. The significance of this to me is that no particular fold of the eight-fold path takes priority over another. Therefore, there is no particular fold that one should begin a discussion with, or focus on first. Having said that, here is an introduction to the eight folds in the order that they are typically presented.

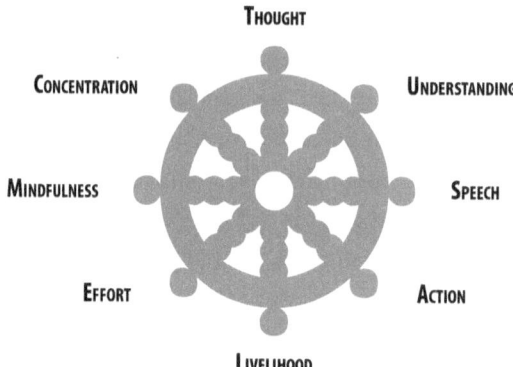

## Wisdom Group

1. **Right Thought** – we should have thoughts of love, non-violence, though without obsession or attachment;
2. **Right Understanding** – we should strive to understand things as they truly are, including the ideas related to Buddhist philosophy;

## Ethical Conduct Group

3. **Right Speech** – we should abstain from talk that is deceiving, backstabbing, slanderous, creates disharmony, is rude, malicious, abusive, idle, or useless;
4. **Right Action** – we should act is a way that honourable and promotes peace and harmony; we should abstain from stealing, dishonest dealings, violence, and improper sexual activity;
5. **Right Livelihood** – we should abstain from a livelihood that brings harm to others;

## Mental Discipline Group

6. **Right Effort** – we should cultivate an approach to life that is positive and enthusiastic, though balanced;
7. **Right Mindfulness** – as we live and act, we should be aware of the sensations we experience, our responses to those sensations, and the thoughts that arise;
8. **Right Concentration** – we should strive to be able to quiet our mind to allow our mind to focus on the object of our attention, such as an idea or physical object, and to come to see it and understand it as it truly is.

There are a couple of things worth noting about this introduction to Buddhism. First, there is no reference to shaving one's head, wearing a robe, and living the life of a monk in a temple. Yet, many associate that image so closely with Buddhism that they believe that to be a Buddhist one must behave like that. A Buddhist monk is like a Christian monk, as a Buddhist minister is like a Roman Catholic Priest, an Islamic Imam, or a Jewish Rabbi. These are all examples of individuals who are committing to a particular expression of their belief system. A great number of Roman Catholics choose to express their belief system by attending church from time to time, or subscribing to specific ideals, or understanding the world as they see it in a particular way. They are not expected to become priests as a requirement of their religious experience, just as a Buddhist is not expected to live as a monk.

Second, the eight-fold path mostly encourages behaviour, rather than prohibits behaviour. It does not focus on what thou-shall-not do. As an ethicist, this is extremely important to me. A set of rules that prohibits behaviour communicates what one should not do, but does not often do a meaningful job of communicating what one should do. Ideas are more useful to me if those ideas help me decide what I should do. While this assessment of the eight-fold path is generally true, the Right Livelihood path has tended to be a bit of an exception.

As a person with a particularly acute interest in business and ethics, I recall being surprised, and then extremely intrigued, by the idea that a religion would place so prominently in its introductory materials a reference to the significance of what we do in the course of making a living, and of engaging in a work environment. I could not recall from my introductions to other religions (in my childhood, or in university) this nod to a matter that I considered to be extremely important. In retrospect, it is ironic that this particular topic should have prompted me to continue my studies of Buddhism, because, as I would come to learn, the topic of Right Livelihood actually receives relatively little effort and attention. Moreover, much of what I did find on this topic was not particularly insightful or useful. So, while I continued to read and study, and learn much more about Buddhism, I was consistently disappointed by the lack of effort and depth on Right Livelihood.

Initially, my sense was that writers and thinkers on the topic of Right Livelihood were just not trying very hard. The evidence for this, I felt, came from the significant difference in the number of pages in a typical book committed to this topic. Pages committed to more popular aspects of the eight-fold path, such as those associated with meditative practices, were numerous. I recall being

## Right Livelihood

disheartened when I would learn that a respected teacher would essentially reduce Right Livelihood to not more than a summary of Right Speech and Right Act. I wondered: if Right Livelihood was meant to be merely a sub-category of Right Speech or Right Act, then why was it presented with its own spoke on the eight-fold wheel?

Sometimes these teachers would speak about Right Livelihood in negative terms. That is, they would say that Right Livelihood was about not saying or doing things that would result in harm, reduce happiness, and increase suffering. However, this approach did not help me decide what I should do as an employee, boss or business owner. For example, I could sit in my basement, drink beer, and play video games (which I actually like to do), and feel some confidence that I was not increasing the amount of unhappiness in the world. However, I am certainly not increasing the amount of happiness in the world, at least not in any meaningful way. I have come to feel that Right Livelihood concepts could include a challenge to Buddhists to aspire to much more than not doing harm.

On the rare occasion that I would come across what was presented as a dedicated effort to the topic of Right Livelihood, and presented as a guide to determining what one should actually do in a work environment, I was again disappointed. I would find that the thinker did not have the level of experience and understanding in the area of business, success, and wealth, to provide me with the degree of value I was looking for.

I have since become far more sympathetic of those writers and thinkers. I have come to accept that topics related to businesses can be extremely difficult for many, and the opportunity to personally create employment opportunities, or excel as an entrepreneur, or achieve financial independence entirely on one's own steam, or mentor others to their own successes, can be rare. Moreover, to those who manage these accomplishments, such a concerted and prolonged effort, with a specific mindset, are so often required that sufficient time or mental inclination for an attempt at a contribution to philosophy is unlikely. That is to say, most who are adept at achieving financial success, and do so with ethics and integrity, are not those that would necessarily engage in teaching about their efforts.

Despite this acceptance, I have come to feel quite strongly that the topic of Right Livelihood should be addressed more prominently by Buddhist scholars, philosophers, the community of Buddhists, and its leaders. This topic is arguably the most important of the eight-fold path, and currently the most worthy of renewed attention and effort. There are at least three good reasons for this.

First, there is an extraordinary opportunity for scholars to consider and compare the historical significance of Right Livelihood with its contemporary significance. Whatever livelihood might have meant, and the activity it might have comprised, thousands of years ago, it is most likely that, for a great number of Buddhists, those activities have changed notably, and will continue to do so. This is made most clear when livelihood, as human behaviour, is compared to the other sorts of behaviour discussed or alluded to in the other folds of the eight-fold path. The mind, for example, has not evolved so much in two thousand years that the core ideas associated with meditation are in danger of being irrelevant. I imagine that the conditions and the human behaviour that might have prompted a philosopher to consider moral prescription regarding thought, speech, and action two thousand years ago may be similar to conditions and behaviour today.

A key feature of the evolution of livelihood activities, as they relate to a matter of ethics, is the distance between that behaviour and the results of the behaviour. Over time, it has become increasingly difficult to determine the effect our livelihood behaviour has on others, or even on ourselves. Historically, livelihood might have featured tilling a garden, then trading vegetables for a chicken with another member of our tribe. Or perhaps making a basket or a spear, and trading those with a stranger who has fish. In these cases, the distance, both geographic and temporal, between the behaviour and the impact of the behaviour is very close. The impact that behaviour might reasonably be expected to have is relatively easy to assess. As such, we might say that it is relatively easy to assess the rightness of that livelihood. That is, it is relatively easy to determine how happiness is increased by that livelihood behaviour.

Of course, today we have a global economy. The production of an item you purchase and use may originate with gathering natural resources, such as minerals. This gathering may take place in variety of countries and involve a variety of people subject to a variety of work conditions. Production is likely to require energy that could come in a variety of forms, from various parts of the world, involving the employment of additional people. Pieces may be then assembled by others in a different location, shipped by various means and persons, stored in various places, and then made available to the consumer by systems requiring additional participants, subject to different work conditions. Can one separate the role of any specific person in this process, and clearly identify the effect of their specific livelihood activity? The distance between one's livelihood behaviour and the impact of that behaviour on others, and even themselves, is both geographically and temporally vast.

This phenomenon of our modern world, and its complexity, present a wonderful opportunity for contemporary Buddhists and philosophers to revisit the topic of Right Livelihood and bring new perspectives to the discussion.

Second, I believe that livelihood-related topics are of interest to the general population. So much of our waking life is given up to the task of receiving education so that we can participate in meaningful employment and careers, and then seeking to fulfil that potential by working. When we are not earning, much of the remaining time is spent spending, and, if we are fortunate, saving. A religion that can address an activity of such significance, and with useful and satisfying guidance, has the opportunity to attract the attention of potential initiates. Like many religions and schools of thought that have endured through time, Buddhism has the potential to evolve, and present itself to new audiences.

My own participation in the Buddhist community has included many years in a leadership capacity, including local, regional and international conferences. I have participated in numerous discussions regarding the past, the present and the future of Buddhism in North America. Like other religious practices and traditions, those associated with Buddhism came to the West with immigrants. For many, their culture and their ethnic community is still strongly associated with their religion. However, as the original immigrants pass on, and the next generation's sense of cultural affiliation becomes less dependent upon their ancestor's country of origin, Buddhist organizations seem to be struggling to keep that next generation engaged.

At the same time, there are others in North America who have no cultural connection with Buddhist philosophy, and may find the religion of their ancestors unable to satisfy all of their intellectual and emotional needs. What is common to of all of these is the significance of livelihood-related activities in their lives. It is here that the emerging Western expression of Buddhism may attract a new generation of participants: by offering them a pursuit of happiness that is consistent with their contemporary experience of living.

There is a third reason that the topic of Right Livelihood requires more attention than it typically receives. Almost every person alive will have to pursue a means of support or subsistence, or a way of making money to live and survive. This might mean being a farmer, eating what you grow, and thereby benefitting directly. The farmer's ability to sustain one's self is a livelihood that reduces their own suffering (like hunger), and increases their own happiness. Certainly, Buddhism, and the eight-fold path, and Right Livelihood are about helping a person have a better, happier life.

However, contemporary Buddhism is seen as being much more than merely a self-serving philosophy. It is understood that the ideals of Buddhism are, more importantly, about helping others. Many of us will pursue our livelihood by working at a job for a company, or will become a professional, or will start our own business of some kind. The work that we do will almost certainly involve others, such as bosses, coworkers, customers, or clients. We will learn that our livelihood is about trying to increase our own happiness, while increasing the happiness of others. Moreover, as I will argue throughout this book, Right Livelihood can be best understood as being about increasing our own happiness by increasing the happiness of others. That is: by focusing on livelihood activities that increase the happiness of others, an increase in our own happiness can be a direct result.

As such, this fold of the eight-fold path, more than any other, has the potential to fulfil its purpose to a degree significantly greater than the others. As a means to reduce or eliminate want, for the reduction of unhappiness, or lessening of suffering, Right Livelihood provides the possibility of benefitting others on a global scale. To be fair, livelihood-related activities can also cause unhappiness and suffering on a global scale as well – which is why getting livelihood-related activities right is so important.

It is not my objective in this book to have you come to accept any of my assessment of Right Livelihood concepts, or these introductory ideas about Buddhist philosophy, as accurate or true. It is my intent, however, to have you come to believe that many of these ideas are useful. Right Livelihood can be more than just one of eight prescriptions in the pursuit of happiness. It can be the one that changes the world. To appreciate this possibility, one must come to understand business endeavours from a particular perspective. The reduction of unhappiness, and the increase of happiness, can be closely associated with morally appropriate work-related behaviour, as well as the realization of personal success and wealth creation. In this respect, these ideas can be very useful indeed. I will explore these ideas next.

# 3
# Success and Wealth

Have you ever caught yourself looking with prolonged interest at a person in a nice, expensive car? Or at a person with expensive clothes, or with a nice home? Or perhaps you see someone on social media posting about an adventurous and exciting holiday? How do you feel at that time? Are you envious? What do you think of those people? Do you think they are successful? If so, how do you feel about that success?

There tends to be a wide range of responses to signs of financial success. Noticing your own response, can be a useful exercise. Why you respond a certain way may help you gain some insight about yourself, and how you feel about money. This may also provide some insight into why you behave as you do. While it is not my intent to convince you to feel a certain way, I do believe that some responses are more useful than others.

For example, I have noticed that some respond to the apparent financial success of others with feelings of negativity about those people. There is a view, for example, that financially successful people have accomplished that state at the expense of others. Perhaps they have achieved that success by deceiving clients or cheating customers. Perhaps they pay their staff poorly, treat them without respect for labour laws or their legal rights, or cut costs which cause unsafe work environment. Perhaps they even engage in criminal activity, like selling drugs or evading taxes. Even if their apparent success is achieved by ethical means, some will respond negatively: "Certainly they have spent too much time working, and not enough time looking after their health, family and community!

Their priorities are messed up!"

These negative responses may represent an increase of unhappiness in the respondent. Armed with only a modest introduction to Buddhist philosophy, one might conclude that this response arises form some form of want or desire. Our want could certainly be associated with some pretty unpleasant states: like envy, jealousy, or even sour grapes. We may want what they have. Accordingly, one might be inclined to encourage the respondent to reduce or eliminate that unhappiness by reducing or eliminating that desire. However, with that, we might end up throwing the baby out with the bathwater. That is: one may choose to pursue that increase in happiness by choosing to lessen one's own desire for success. Is this a particularly useful approach? I associate this approach with what a Buddhist might refer to as the lesser vehicle – a Buddhist approach to unhappiness that produces lesser results. In this case, the target result is the reduction of unhappiness of a single person, by eliminating a want or desire in that person. In contrast, the greater vehicle may be understood as a Buddhist approach to unhappiness that produces greater results. This is a more aspirational application of Buddhist philosophy that considers the possibility of assisting a greater number of people to experience more happiness. Sometimes, I imagine an actual vehicle (like a motorcycle) that can take a single person on a journey, and compare that to a larger vehicle (like a bus) that can take many. Perhaps this response to the phenomenon of success could be more useful. How would this work?

I have been most fortunate in my professional work to have met and worked with a large number of people whom I would consider to be successful. Many of these were colleagues and competitors in the financial services industry. Many were my clients, who were pursuing and achieving success with a wide range of endeavours. Others engaged in complementary professions, and assisted me with my work, such as lawyers and accountants. As I began to write, and then speak at conferences, I was introduced to even more (and sometimes famous) successful people. From their successes and perspectives on what it means to be successful, I received some very useful guidance.

As a result, I have come to understand success, in the simplest terms, to be about setting and achieving goals. While some goals may be common (like having a family, or a nice home), many will have goals that are less common, or particularly meaningful to them. The variety of goals, and the priority in which goals are pursued, reflect the variety of values that influence behaviour. Thinking about success in these terms (rather than about owning a fancy car, or designer clothes) is useful because it can help us to focus on the skills and perspectives we need to develop that may increase the likelihood of being successful ourselves.

We can increase the likelihood of being successful by improving our goal-setting skills. For example, some subscribe to the notion of setting SMART goals, where SMART is an acronym for: Specific, Measurable, Action-orientated, Realistic, and Timebound. They would report that setting goals with these features will increase the likelihood of achieving success. Others will also suggest that we can further increase our likelihood of success by what we do after we set our goals, for example: write down our SMART goals, reflect on them with regularity, note and celebrate our progress, and share our goals with others.

Nevertheless, setting goals, however SMART, will not assure success. John Landy had a goal. His goal was to win a very specific race. In that race was his rival, Roger Bannister. Each had managed to accomplish what was, in its day, a very remarkable feat. Each had completed a one mile race in less than four minutes, and they were the only men known to have done so. On May 6th, 1954, Bannister ran one mile in 3 minutes and 59.4 seconds, which set a world record. This time was bettered less than two months later by Landy, who set a new record by running one mile in 3 minutes and 58 seconds. In August of the same year, with the world watching, the two met in Vancouver to compete, and to determine who was fastest.

As the now legendary story goes, Landy and Bannister were running shoulder to shoulder throughout the race. As they neared the finish line, Landy managed to establish a small, but definite lead, and it began to look as if he (the current world record holder) would confirm his status as fastest man in the world. Yet, just steps before the finish line, Landy turns his head slightly to look for his competitor. With that distraction, Bannister seizes the opportunity for one final burst of speed, and passes Landy on the other side to victory. There is a statue near the site of that famous race which immortalizes both Bannister's accomplishment and the look of pain and disappointment on Landy's face.

Photo: Paul Joseph, Wikimedia Commons

Why was Landy unsuccessful that day? Did he not have a goal? Certainly he did. He had a very clear goal: to win the race, to beat Bannister, to confirm his status as the world's fastest human. We could even say that this was a SMART goal. It was specific: to be the first to the finish line. It was measurable: running a distance of exactly one mile. It was action-orientated: broken down into specific, individual steps. It was realistic: he was the world record holder at the time. It was time-bound: ideally, complete the race in less than four minutes. There must be something more to this business of being successful than merely being a competent goal-setter.

As the story of Landy and Bannister demonstrates, there are two primary types of goals. Competitive goals, for example, are goals we set that require another to fail in the pursuit of their goal. This is known as a zero-sum equation. Our win implies another's loss. We see it in sporting events, of course, like a one-mile foot race. All the runners are pursuing victory, with more failing in the attempt than achieving success. We also see this in other forms of human behaviour, like livelihood endeavours. Achieving the goal of being top sales person will require that others are unsuccessful in that pursuit. Winning a legal victory will often require that another other party does not. Due to scarcity of resources, or limitations of a market place, it can be expected that not every business will survive; the success of the survivor often comes at the expense of the failed effort. Like the natural world of flora and fauna, the business world may become populated by those enterprises most fit.

In contrast, positive goals are the goals that we set for which success is measured by other parties also accomplishing their goals. This is known as a win-win equation. Early in my career as a sales person of financial products and services, I would measure my success by the amount of product sold, and the amount revenue generated, as compared to my peers. I received awards, accolades and promotions – each because my colleagues and competitors produced results that were deemed inferior to my own. As such, I learned to set competitive goals, and I was positively reinforced by my employers for doing so. This approach and perspective, however, brought me limited success, and a limited sense of fulfilment. When I began to focus on positive goals, and on measuring my success by the success of others, I began to experience my livelihood in a new and more fulfilling way.

I came to recognize that positive goals can have an advantage over competitive goals, and this advantage arises from the types of relationships that are formed in each goal environment.

With competitive goals come competitive relationships. Since, in this environment, our success comes at the expense of another, the relationships we form actively seek to undermine our efforts. With positive goals, positive relationships are formed, and we become encouragers of, and stakeholders in, each other's success. By shifting my focus from competitive goal-setting to positive goal-setting, and focusing my attention on the positive relationships that would arise, I began to experience new forms of achievement. I began to recognize that I could work in an environment of interdependence, and began to attract clients, colleagues and other professionals who were like-minded. They would actively work to help me become more successful because I was working to make them more successful.

Buddhist philosophy contributes to this perspective of interdependence, albeit in some pretty abstract ways. One of the concepts that can seem most foreign to newer students of the tradition is the idea of no self. This idea proposes that the sense that there is a self, an I, that is distinct and separate from what we experience is an illusion. This is related to the Buddhist notion of non-duality – the proposition that we are not meaningfully separate from what we experience. These ideas may be discussed as a matter of physics. In other words, one could propose that we are not really separate from what is around us in a physical way. This sort of discussion of the metaphysical is an attempt to describe a true reality, beyond what we may perceive. For philosophy students, this was considered to be an interesting topic to ponder over beers, but arguably not of much use beyond that. I have since become far more interested in the idea of non-duality and interdependence as it pertains to ethics – as it pertains to what should be, rather than to what is. Understanding our behaviour, especially our goal-setting and goal-pursuing behaviour, as being interconnected with the behaviour of others, is both morally and practically useful. From a moral perspective, it suggests that we should be mindful of how we act to hurt or to benefit another, since, because of our interdependence, we are also acting to hurt or benefit our self. Moreover, the idea is useful as it better enables us to set and achieve our goals, through a recognition of positive relationships. A full appreciation of the interconnectedness of our existence helps us arrive at a useful perspective: by helping others to become successful we are directly creating our own success. When we help others to truly benefit, we will truly benefit ourselves.

I refer to this true benefit as value. Giving value that is a true benefit should be the desired objective of livelihood activities. Put another way, Right Livelihood results from the receipt of value by the object of that behaviour, as well as by the subject. For example, I would not personally sell cigarettes for my livelihood. Even if it helps the consumer accomplish their goal (like satisfying their need arising from addiction), and it helps me accomplish my goal (like making money to buy food), I do not see this as providing a true benefit, or real value, to the consumer. In fact, from this idea of interconnectedness, as I contribute to the harm experienced by the consumer, I will experience harm myself. This harm may come in very tangible ways: social ills, added costs to a health care system, a loss of productivity due to illness, general unhappiness, etc. True success will result from helping others achieve goals that result in the realization of true value.

Value that is provided when engaging in Right Livelihood may come in different forms. Addressing and satisfying human needs is an example of giving value. We need food and shelter to survive, and business activities that satisfy those needs are providing value. We also have wants that may not be needs. For example, we may feel a desire for entertainment or to have some inconvenience eliminated. Again, these are opportunities for those engaged in related livelihoods to help others to receive value. As I advanced in my own career, and gained additional business experiences, I began to understand success as being measured by the extent to which I had helped others successfully gain value.

There is a very specific way that we can measure that type of success in our society: money.

Money can be understood as a measurement of the amount of value that has been provided, and the significance of that value. For example, a very talented surgeon, who can save a life with their rare surgical skills, can be understood to be providing value to his or her patient. The work is so exhausting and stressful that the surgeon only operates a few times per week, but the value is so significant that the surgeon is paid very well. The surgeon may achieve a specific type of success: financial success. This success may be evident to others in the form of fancy clothes and an expensive car, but is derived from helping others to be successful in the pursuit of their goal (not dying). Providing a cup of coffee is also an example of providing value. This is a value that does not require a very specific or hard-to-learn skill, and is provided by many and in volume. Other than some calories, some stimulation, a break from work, or an opportunity for social interaction, the value is not very significant, and the remuneration for the cup of coffee is fairly modest. Yet, if this value is given to enough people, on enough occasions, financial success can be realized.

Financial success can be understood as a by-product of giving value in the right combination of sufficient significance and sufficient volume. That value is related to increasing happiness, or reducing suffering, on the part of the person who receives that value. Right Livelihood, therefore, is about providing value, and can be seen as an ethical way of achieving financial success.

As with other forms of success, the likelihood of achieving financial success can be increased by improving our goal-setting skills, by emphasising positive goals, and by focusing on the positive relationships that arise. Thinking in terms of how we provide value to others in these pursuits will increase the likelihood of success even more. For example, suppose that you have a goal to be a millionaire. You might improve the likelihood of achieving this objective if you practiced SMART with your goal setting. So, be specific: have a $1 million dollar net worth. Be measurable: have $50,000 in cash, $250,000 in securities, and $700,000 in real estate.

Be action-orientated: save $2,500 per year as cash, invest $10,000 in securities per year, purchase and pay off a home. Be realistic: understand and confirm your income, expenses, and budget to determine if the goal is possible. Be time-bound: to be completed in 20 years. Thinking in terms of how we can help others accomplish their goals and to become successful, to provide them value, will help us focus on how we can earn the income that will be required to fund our goal. By focusing on the positive relationships that arise, we can consider how to collaborate in the delivery of that value for mutual benefit.

For some, when thinking about their goals for financial success, they tend to focus on the outcome and the rewards. When they think about this success, they are really wondering about what it would be like to have fancy clothes and an expensive car. They think about how they will feel, or about how they hope others will feel when they see them in their fancy clothes and expensive car. While it is all well and good to be motivated, the goal setter will find that they are more likely to realize those outcomes if they are focused on the process required to get there. They should be asking:

- What value can I currently provide?
- What is the significance of that value?
- What volume of value will I need to provide?
- Can I provide that volume?
- Can I increase the significance of the value I can provide?
- Should I be increasing my skills, receiving training, or pursuing more education?
- What do I need to do to be able to provide enough value to receive the reward I need to accomplish my goal?

When approached in this way, not only does the pursuit of financial success seem to be morally acceptable, but it could also been seen as an obligation. If the livelihood we pursue is right, in the sense that we are focused on providing value to others, and that value is measured as an increase in happiness and reduction in suffering, then should we not be obliged to pursue it? If by providing real value to others we also receive financial compensation sufficient to accomplish our own goals, increase our own happiness, and reduce our own suffering, should we not be obliged to do so?

For some, these ideas may seem reasonable, and yet they will be concerned that one might take these ideas as justification to go too far. They may accept the notion that it is morally acceptable, perhaps even obligatory, to pursue enough financial success to satisfy one's needs, or the needs of their family, but would caution that this is a slippery slope. They may argue, for example, that in the pursuit of such success, some might get greedy, and pursue more than they need. They are concerned, perhaps, specifically by those that pursue and achieve wealth.

Wealth is a special type of financial success. It is not merely about having enough money and resources; it is about having more than enough. The pursuit and realization of wealth is seen by some as an example of the moral decay of a person, or even as a sign of the moral decay of a society that reveres such pursuits. Some may see the achievement of wealth as a gain for some that necessarily results from the loss to others. While I would freely admit that some gain wealth in this way, it is most certainly not true of all, and, at any rate, it is not a very useful way to view this phenomenon.

Wealth can also result from having provided a significant amount of value to a significant number of people. Some of the world's wealthiest individuals, families and businesses have produced this result by doing some very remarkable things, or by contributing to the creation of some extraordinarily impactful products and services. The technology sector has provided many noteworthy examples of life-changing devices that have transformed our society. Some in the entertainment industry have achieved unusual personal wealth, by giving millions of experiences of enjoyment to others – one song, one movie, one game at a time. Wealth may be seen as the by-product of one's ability to provide a very unusual form of value to a very unusual number of people. It is important to remember, however, that this is unusual, by definition.

## Success and Wealth

Wealthy is an adjective that describes a state of affairs the meaningfulness of which is dependent upon there being other states of affairs. In this regard, it is like the adjective tall. For there to be a person aptly described as tall, there must be another who is not. The idea of tall has sense because we have an idea of short. Imagine for a moment that every person that existed was exactly the same height. Would the word tall have any useful meaning? Or imagine that there is only one person left alive in the universe, and everyone else is long dead and decayed. Is that person tall or short? It is useful to think of wealthy in the same way.

For someone to be considered wealthy, there must be others who are not. Imagine that a single person had a million dollars and everyone else alive had less that one thousand dollars. I would feel comfortable in describing that person as wealthy. However, if everyone alive had one million dollars, I would not describe anyone as wealthy. If there were one person left alive, and that person had all the money, and all the resources, I would not describe that person as wealthy. Understanding wealth and wealthy in this way is useful because it can help us to better understand how we may want to behave when it comes to our livelihood and financial aspirations. It suggests to me, that if we want to achieve wealth – the accumulation of more than enough money and resources – we should be prepared to strive to provide more value than others provide.

It also suggests to me that, try as we might, not everyone will achieve wealth, because the definition precludes that possibility. This perspective is contrary to the message articulated by many in the you too can be rich self-help businesses. There are some who will give the impression that everyone can achieve wealth…if those people just follow their program, adhere to their financial planning advice, or read their book. In fact, by definition, a typical person will produce a typical amount of value for others and realize a typical amount of financial success. By definition, half the human population can be expected to produce value of less than the average and realize financial success less than the average.

Those who want to experience atypical financial success to the point of achieving wealth would be advised to consider how they can deliver an atypical, much-more-than-the-average amount of value to others. To do this, they should consider their livelihood. When I worked as a financial advisor, and then as a manager, and then as a business owner, I would have conversations wherein a person, a couple, or a business owner, would share with me their financial aspirations. They could picture and describe what that meant to them: enough money and investment income so that they did not have to work, a big, beautiful home in the most expensive community, world-class holidays, etc. I would consider their situation, and think to myself: "I am sorry, but you can't get there from here." That is: many of these were folks engaged in some pretty normal occupations, and providing some pretty average amounts of value, but hoping that these efforts would result in unusual financial success.

Consider a barber, for example. That barber cuts one head of hair at a time, and only for so many hours per day. While I would imagine that some barbers are more talented than others, the ability to cut hair is not a particularly difficult skill, and the cost of entry into that line of work is not particularly high. As such, there is much competition. The opportunity for wealth creation from barbering seems to be pretty limited. Although, a barber could hire additional barbers, or franchise their business, or create a line of hair products, or speculate with investments, or win the lottery, or inherit a fortune, and end up wealthy. In these cases, wealth was not created by being a barber, it was created by being an employer, by being a business owner, by being an entrepreneur, or perhaps just being lucky. I have never met a wealthy barber *per se*.

To be clear, it is certainly acceptable to provide an average amount of value and realize an average amount of financial success. If pursued with an interest in increasing happiness and reducing suffering, then that may be an excellent example of Right Livelihood. Moreover, the world needs this kind of average. Without average, above average has no meaning. Without average, there would

## Success and Wealth

be no opportunity for those motivated to provide an above-average effort, in an attempt to deliver above-average value, and ultimately realize above-average success. For this reason, I welcome and appreciate all who earnestly pursue Right Livelihood regardless of their financial aspirations. Yet, I admire those who have attempted to deliver that unusual amount of value. Even if they do not realize the specific success that they sought, the effort they made, the risks they took, and the commitment to becoming the person that they would need to become, is often most inspirational.

I do not propose that one would have an obligation to be wealthy. To the extent that achieving wealth is a by-product of one's ability to provide an unusual degree of value to an unusual number of people, then perhaps we at least have an obligation to try. Being envious of the person with the nice car, nice home, financial success, and even wealth, and responding by reducing our own desires is not particularly useful. We should be envious that they have the skills, the dedication, and the ability to give value that produces that kind of success. This desire should inspire us to also attain the skills, muster the dedication, and realize the abilities to give a value of such significance to such number as to produce similar results. Rather than take the lesser way, and merely reduce our own wants, we can take the greater way, and seek to reduce the wants of others.

# 4
# Entrepreneurship and Value Delivery

Regardless of your current personal goals, motivations and aspirations, and the degree to which they may include the pursuit of financial success, you will most likely find yourself engaged in livelihood in an organization that is attempting to provide value. This may be an organization that you have created as an entrepreneur, or it may be an organization created by others. Let's now consider Right Livelihood from the perspective of an entrepreneur, how value delivery systems are formed, and how you may see your role in these systems. The parable of Siddhartha Gautama is a good place to start.

Said to have been born in Nepal (sometime between the 6th and 4th century BCE), Siddhartha Gautama was a spiritual leader and teacher whose life is associated with the foundation of Buddhism. According to lore, he was a Prince who lived a sheltered life, with little experience beyond the walls of his palace – until one day he ventured forth and was confronted with the suffering of people. He decided to leave the comforts of his home, determined to find a way to reduce suffering and increase happiness. He would spend many years of dedicated efforts and self-sacrifice in this pursuit, before becoming awakened to the solution. He then shared his solution in the form of teachings, and as an example with his practice. Siddhartha, the Buddha, is an archetypical entrepreneur.

The entrepreneur is a person who identifies problems and seeks to find solutions. The entrepreneur sees shortcomings and imperfections, and pursues opportunities to provide improvements. Sometimes the solutions come in the form of relatively minor adjustments to a product or a service, but which can result in a meaningful increase of value provided by those products and services. In other cases, completely new products or services are conceptualized that solve problems in a way the previous solutions did not. In rarer instances, a new product or service is introduced that increases happiness or reduces suffering for the benefit of millions of people, and seems to change the world. Further, it may not be uncommon for an entrepreneur to commit to extraordinary and prolonged efforts, as well as considerable personal sacrifice, in these pursuits. From this perspective, entrepreneurial endeavours have three distinct features:

- **Awareness**: A recognition of a need to fulfil, a problem to solve, or of an opportunity for improvement.
- **Motivation**: A desire to increase happiness and reduce suffering.
- **Effort**: A commitment to finding the solution to the problem.

Some problems are fairly easy to recognize, as the human needs that generate these problems are common. Abraham Maslow is probably the best known articulator of these human needs. His paper, *A Theory of Motivation* (1943), states that people are motivated to achieve certain needs, and some needs take precedence over others. That is: we tend to look after the more basic, fundamental needs before moving on to more advanced needs; we pursue the got to have before moving on to the nice to have. Here are those needs, ascending according to Maslow's Pyramid:

1. First, **Physiological** needs: the need humans have in order to sustain and perpetuate life. These are said to include: air, water, food, shelter/clothing, sleep, and reproduction.
2. Then, **Safety** needs: personal security, employment,

## Entrepreneurship and Value Delivery

resources, health, and property.
3. Then, **Love** and belonging: friendship, intimacy, family, sense of connection.
4. Then, **Esteem**: respect, self-esteem, recognition, strength, freedom.
5. Then, **Self-actualization**: desire to become the most that one can be.

It is useful to think of these needs as they relate to states such as suffering or happiness. When the basic needs are not met, such as food, water and shelter, we may find that the person is suffering. When less basic needs are not met, such as a need for recognition, the person may not be best described as suffering, but could just be described as unfulfilled, or not as happy as they could be. Livelihood activities of the entrepreneur can range from a desire to reduce or eliminate suffering to increasing happiness in varying degrees.

These are very useful distinctions for the would-be entrepreneur. Since everyone shares the physiological needs, the size of the market for products and services that fulfill these needs and solve related problems, is theoretically very, very large. Where there is a large market, and where the need is necessary for survival, and where suffering may result if the need is not fulfilled, solving those problems can result in the delivery of a significant amount of value. This, in turn, could result in the realization of a considerable amount of financial success for the entrepreneur. However, because of this, the number of people attempting to provide such products and services can also be very, very large. So, competition is stiff. Yet, clever entrepreneurs continue to find opportunity for improvement, and opportunity to bring value to the market.

Other entrepreneurs may be attracted to addressing less fundamental needs. The farther along the continuum of these needs, to needs such as belonging, esteem and self-actualization, the less motivation there may be on the part of the consumer for the solutions being offered. Since they are not suffering from their unmet need, the potential value is perhaps less significant, as it is in the pursuit of increasing happiness. Yet, with much of the world now able to have their most basic survival needs satisfied, the interest in, and market for, the satisfaction of the less basic needs may be growing. The prevalence of interest in social media, for example, maybe understood as humans attempting to satisfy the needs of love and belonging (friendship, sense of connection) and the need to realize positive self-esteem (respect, recognition), or even the possibility of self-actualization (finding the perfect employment opportunity, for example). Though this form of value may be relatively insignificant (when compared, for example, to the products and services that are necessary for supporting life), the number of persons receiving the value is very high. Currently, some of the world's most financially successful entrepreneurs are engaged in livelihoods associated with these business opportunities, or related software and hardware.

Most human needs, regardless of the significance, are being addressed in one way or another – if not by another entrepreneur, then perhaps by an established business, a government organization, or a not-for-profit. Completely new solutions to old problems are rare. As such, to be successful, entrepreneurs have to be creative. One such form of creativity is represented when existing solutions are combined in novel ways to solve problems differently. Even in well-established industries and professions, a form of entrepreneurial spirit can manifest, and livelihood pursuits can include a fresh approach, with evolving perspectives. I had such an experience with a business that I formed, called Canadians Retiring Abroad.

The financial services industry provides livelihood opportunities for hundreds of thousands of Canadians, including well over 100,000 registrants that are permitted to provide investments. Many of these serve a market of prospective and current retirees. It is a very competitive industry, and does not easily support an individual's innovation and creativity. In this environment, I and a couple of entrepreneurial colleagues decided that we would try to be the exception to the rule. At this point in my career, I had been primarily employed by, or contracted with, large, well-known financial institutions, with established brands, and rigid systems. I was typically self-employed in the sense that my compensation was based fully on commission, I was responsible for most of my own expenses, and I had some flexibility as to where and when I worked. However, it felt much more like I was a franchisee: being bound by the processes and business models created by others. Despite my successes in this environment, I desired the opportunity to identify problems, and craft solutions, with my own sense of entrepreneurial spirit. Additionally, I was extremely motivated to spend more time travelling abroad. I wondered whether or not there was a way to combine the two interests.

I began to study the topic of international retirement. I came to realize that there was wide range of often-complicated issues facing those that wanted to have an extended adventure in retirement, as a snowbird, or even as an expatriate (a person resident abroad). Many of these topics were not covered in the educational programs for typical investment advisors and retirement planners, and so solutions to the related issues were typically not readily available to consumers. My colleagues and I decided to offer a specialized, holistic, retirement planning service specifically for this market, under the name Canadians Retiring Abroad. From this effort, I learned some of the basic principles of entrepreneurship. One of these is to establish points of differentiation. This is especially critical when it comes to seeking the opportunity to provide novel solutions to problems that are already being tackled by competing providers. Differentiation, I realized, comes in three forms: differentiation by purpose, by product, and by process.

Differentiation by purpose refers to the ability of the entrepreneur to address the consumer's purpose or objective in a way not currently being addressed by other service providers. While the financial services industry as a whole provides countless services to provide value to a consumer preparing for, transitioning to, or attempting to enjoy retirement in general (often undefined) terms, we focused on a very specific type of retirement experience. The specificity of this differentiation also meant we could more clearly identify, describe, and communicate to our target audience. We knew that we were seeking to give value to a more adventurous, and perhaps a bit more rebellious, submarket. Consumers in this market, we estimated, by their very nature, would be more open to learning about a new and unusual service provider.

Differentiation by product refers to the ability of the entrepreneur to develop and introduce a new component to a service, like a new product. Offering a new product can be exceedingly difficult in a very old, large, and established industry. Yet, we recognized a need among our market that was both significant and not being effectively addressed. One of the concerns for an aging person, living outside of Canada, is health care. The more familiar solutions to health and emergency needs (such as public health services, travel insurance, long-term care insurance, critical illness insurance) have short-comings for non-resident retirees. As such, Canadians Retiring Abroad worked with an insurance organization to create a group health care plan for this market. To the best of my knowledge, this was the first such product of its kind specifically for Canadians.

Differentiation by process refers to the ability of the entrepreneur to attract and engage the market in unique and compelling ways. As a rule of thumb, this is the easiest of the three forms of differentiation to achieve. In the case of Canadians Retiring Abroad, our service and our market very naturally leant themselves to processes featuring education and the love of travel. For example, we ran a series of educational events in Western Canada on the topic of international retirement. Though a retirement seminar is not an unusual feature of a new client attraction process in the financial services industry, the number of attendees we were able to attract was extremely unusual. Often promoted by little more than an announcement of "Retire to Mexico!" in a newspaper, we attracted as many as 500 prospective clients to a single evening event. Additionally, we took our process to an international market, with educational events in existing communities of Americans and Canadians throughout Mexico. On a few occasions, we organized travel experiences for our Canadian clients and prospects to all-inclusive resorts and on cruises. These included our educational programs, personalized planning meetings, and tours of prospective retirement destinations. Guests paid for their own travel and related expenses. (My previous book, *More Awesome Client Events* chronicles these kinds of activities in more detail).

Another principle of entrepreneurship that I learned from my Canadians Retiring Abroad experience is to understand the distinction between a means value and an ends value. The human needs described by Maslow, for example, feature an end or an outcome directly desired by the human. Products and services that address these needs directly, and thereby increase happiness or reduce suffering directly, can be said to be providing an ends value. A product or service that is readily desired by, and sought out by, a consumer, are more likely to be addressing an ends needs with an ends value.

Think in terms of the so-called bucket list: the list of things a person wants to do before they die. For example, a person may want to take their grandchildren to Disneyland. It is on the bucket list. This may be related to a need to be connected with family, or for recognition from the grandchildren. The trip to Disneyland is a product or service that directly addresses the need and directly results in increased happiness. Such products and services are actively sought out by consumers, and the value as it relates to the need is clearly understood.

However, many products and services do not have this status of being directly addressing a need. These products are a means to an end. The means is not desired in and of itself, but can come to be desired as it may lead to the end – the state of affairs actually desired. In such circumstances, the value of the means may be harder to recognize, as it is less connected to the end need. Consumers are less inclined to actively seek means value unless they clearly see how that value results in the addressing of the actual need. The financial services industry, for example, does not typically provide products and services that are desired in and of themselves. Nowhere in Maslow's list is a need for a pool of public securities managed by a professional. So, the product (or service) of a mutual fund does not directly address a need; it does not provide an end value. We would likely be surprised if a person put on their bucket list: own a mutual fund.

If financial products and services provide value (a topic we will explore in much more detail later), then that value is a means value. They may help the consumer achieve an ends value that is related to a direct need, but much more effort may be required to communicate that potential of that value to the market. For an entrepreneur who wants the market to see the potential for value in their offered product or service, significant benefit can be gained by connecting the value as closely as possible with the need – especially if that value is a means value. With Canadians Retiring Abroad, we were focused on addressing the actual needs, and the bucket list of our clients and prospects. We recognized that no one actually wanted the products and services we provided, but what they wanted was the ends value that could result. So, we stayed focused on the adventure, the desired ends, and the actual needs, rather than the means.

This distinction between the means and the ends, with respect to a value to be delivered, can also be applied to the processes that attempt to deliver that value. This is the distinction between the what the entrepreneur is attempting to accomplish and the how they are attempting to accomplish it. It is useful to consider these processes in terms of the harm they may cause and the good they may cause. The processes that may lead to the delivery of the intended value, and, thereby, the intended increase in happiness, may also lead to other outcomes. These other outcomes may include an increase in suffering and unhappiness. Right Livelihood requires a measurement of both, the potential intended value, as well as the potential harms from the processes. It requires a measurement of

## Entrepreneurship and Value Delivery

the moral appropriateness of both the what and the how.

In the course of your livelihood, you will contribute to the delivery of the value by engaging in the process of its delivery. Indeed, entrepreneurs will often learn very quickly that the ability to deliver the intended value will require the support of others, with various skills – people just like you. You will be part of the how. If you care about the moral appropriateness of your behaviour, and specifically of your ability to engage in Right Livelihood, you will want to consider your role in these processes. Feeling satisfied that the enterprise you are supporting has the potential to reduce suffering and increase happiness through it products and services will not be enough. You will want to consider the moral appropriateness of these processes as well. As the saying goes: the ends does not justify the means. That is, immoral behaviour that ultimately produces some measurable good does not (by itself) justify that behaviour.

Some Buddhist traditions describe non-virtues. These are examples of behaviours considered to be morally inappropriate, even if they happen to be part of a process that may produce some good. These include the prescription to refrain from behaviour associated with: killing; stealing; sexual misconduct; lying; slander; harsh speech; useless speech; covetousness; ill-will; and misguided beliefs. Much of this could be seen as directly covered by, or implied by, the ideas of the Eight-Fold Path (described in Chapter 2). These non-virtues, like their Eight-Fold Path counterparts, have a similar short-coming: merely telling me what I should not do is much less useful than helping me decide what I should do. Some hold the belief that livelihoods resulting in the creation of weapons, intoxicants, and poisons, for example, are always morally inappropriate regardless of the processes. Others hold the view that killing animals is not morally inappropriate in and of itself, but that the moral appropriateness of that activity is determined largely by the processes. As you contemplate your contribution to the value delivery process, a pursuit of Right Livelihood suggests that you will want to consider how your very specific behaviour within the value delivery process leads to the increase of happiness.

I have seen that it can be a challenge for a person engaged in livelihood to see how their contribution fits into the overall process of value delivery. One of the reasons for this is that such systems often feature individuals completing a very specific task. Their task is their focus, and what they do is combined with the tasks being completed by others. A system of individuals specializing in the completing of a specific task is often thought to provide for the most efficient and effective value delivery processes. Unfortunately, by focusing on a specific task, we may not be able to see how that task fits with the others in the delivery of value. We do not clearly see the problems that we are solving, or the happiness to which we are contributing. Additionally, sometimes the entrepreneur who identified the problem, and then worked to formulate a solution, does not do a very good job of imparting the enthusiasm and spirit of their pursuits with those brought in to contribute to the process of the delivery of the value. If you are in that process, you may need to take the initiative yourself to discover what that problem and solution identification activity might have been like for the entrepreneur. This might be as simple as asking the owner of the business some questions. In fact, these are the questions that the entrepreneur may have asked themselves at some point in their endeavours:

- What is the problem we are attempting to solve?
- Why is this a problem worth solving?
- What need or needs are we addressing?
- Is the elimination or reduction of the need related more to eliminating suffering or increasing happiness?
- How is this problem currently being addressed by others?
- Is our solution different from existing solutions?
- How is it different? (By purpose, by product, by process)
- Is the solution more of a means value or an ends value?
- How does the market understand our proposed solution?

## Entrepreneurship and Value Delivery

These questions and answers may help you become aware of the value proposition of your organization, and a better sense of your role in value delivery. They can also help you confirm whether or not you are engaged in Right Livelihood: whether or not you are reducing suffering and unhappiness, and increasing happiness. To be clear, this determination is not based solely on whether or not the organization you work for is providing that value, but whether or not you are contributing meaningfully to the delivery of that value. There may be opportunity or potential for you to contribute meaningfully, but are you in fact doing so? The principle of Right Livelihood dictates that you should be actively giving value, not merely being associated with those that do.

I believe there is a form of mindfulness that can be useful for someone intent on engaging in Right Livelihood. This form of mindfulness is an awareness of what we are doing while we work, who might be harmed by what we are doing, and who might benefit from what we are doing. In the course of doing our work, our mind may wander from the task at hand. Mentally we may drift to unrelated ideas, or to negative, and potentially distracting thoughts. This may happen in a matter of moments, while we are doing one of our regular, perhaps mundane, tasks in the process. It may happen over the course of days, years, or an entire career: our mind drifting away from the value delivery purpose of our work. We lose sight of what we might have known clearly at some point: that our livelihood activity, to be Right Livelihood, must be about how our work is benefitting another. As those who practice meditation have learned, in the course of pursuing our livelihood, there will be times when we must gently bring our attention back to the purpose of our work. Right Livelihood can benefit from this form of mindfulness.

Yet, what if in the course of your questioning, and discovery, and mindfulness at work, you come to believe that the organization you are involved in is not truly focused on the value delivery that you thought it was. Perhaps whatever problem-solving motivation the founders had has dissipated over the years. Perhaps the processes currently used in support of the alleged value proposition are themselves creating harm and unhappiness. What if your colleagues are engaged in crime, bullying or corruption? What if, despite all of that, you are doing your very best to engage in Right Livelihood? From an ethics perspective, you have a problem.

Regardless of how morally appropriate our own task is to a process, if our contribution enables and supports unethical behaviour, the creation of harm, and the increase of unhappiness, we are complicit in those outcomes. In a livelihood environment, we receive our income and other benefits as a result of the overall behaviour of the organization. Indeed, we may benefit in other ways from morally inappropriate livelihood. Speaking as an ethicist, one of my favourite television characters is Carmela Soprano, wife of the notorious Tony Soprano. Carmela lived in a beautiful home, owned nice cars, and enjoyed social prestige. She was able to spend her time looking after her children, lunching with friends, and volunteering for her church. Yet this lifestyle was available because of her husband's significant role in organized crime. This livelihood behaviour produced very significant harm, including injury and death. Carmela benefitted from this behaviour. Indeed, her livelihood was derived directly from this behaviour, and she enabled and supported it. Is she not subject to the same moral judgement as her husband? Could she be engaged in Right Livelihood when her actual livelihood is the result of harm? What of Tony's lawyer, and accountant, and the friend who borrows his boat. What of the local church that may happily receive donations? They also benefit directly from his criminal activity. If you find that you are benefitting from the harm caused by others, you have an obligation either to alter the processes that produce the harm, or seek to contribute to, and benefit from, other processes.

The notion of non-duality has an interesting application here. The idea that we are not really distinct from what is around us, suggests that we should consider carefully what and who we surround of ourselves with. While we are interconnected with others on a

## Entrepreneurship and Value Delivery

global scale, the degree of that interconnectedness is not equally distributed. Those we are closer to, and spend more time with, influence who we are and how we behave more than those at a greater distance. If we are spending time with those who engage in illegal or unethical behaviour, and especially if that behaviour is related to livelihood activity, we are an aspect of that behaviour. We are them. We become as bad as the work environment we chose to be in.

Following that perspective, when you are contributing to, participating in, and benefitting from processes that deliver value, your behaviour is laudable. We can become as good as those around us. Though receiving praise may not be your specific objective, being praiseworthy is certainly one of the many potential positive outcomes and motivations. Over your working life, there may be occasion that you feel that your contribution is not particularly meaningful. Your self-esteem may suffer, as you wonder about the importance of your work, or whether or not anyone actually cares about what you do. These are the moments to practice that mindfulness. Take some time to understand the value proposition of the organization you work in, remind yourself of how others benefit from this work, and how you contribute to that benefit by contributing to the process. Mindfully, bring your thoughts and attention back to your Right Livelihood. Not only does this help you, it helps those around you. As you are interconnected with them, they benefit from your efforts.

As an entrepreneur or as a contributor to the value delivery processes, how you feel about your work is as important as how your customer or client feels when receiving your products or services. Right Livelihood produces symbiotic relationships. Right Livelihood manifests when the needs of all participants are considered and addressed: those receiving and those providing the value. It is not merely the problems and human needs of the consumers to be alleviated, but those of the entrepreneur and the value deliverers as well. Right Livelihood means that you are addressing your own needs, like those described by Maslow. By earning a living, you are able to address your own basic needs, and hopefully will not suffer. Moreover, Right Livelihood provides the means of addressing those less basic needs that result in your increased happiness. These include your needs for belonging, to enjoy positive self-esteem, and realize self-actualization. If you are working in an environment that does not acknowledge and attempt to address your needs, then you are not engaged in Right Livelihood. If you are an entrepreneur, or aspire to be one, you would be wise to put as much effort into the needs of those you want to attract to your growing value delivery process as to your target customers.

The positive outcomes of value delivery can most certainly include the achievement of financial success. Solving problems, reducing suffering, and increasing happiness can often be mutually beneficial. The significance of the value provided, and the number of people experiencing that value, can be a strong indicator of the potential financial reward to the entrepreneur. Others in the value delivery process have the potential to gain financial reward, and the significance of that reward is typically a reflection of the significance of the value that they provide to the process.

As a rule of thumb, the entrepreneur stands to experience more financial success, even to the point of achieving wealth, than others in the process. If you are working for an entrepreneur that has engaged in Right Livelihood, and has achieved wealth as a result, you may experience feelings of jealousy. You may feel that it is somehow not fair that you are working hard in the value delivery process, and only receiving modest financial reward. If that is the case, you are most welcome to become an entrepreneur yourself. Wealth can come from being responsible for providing an unusual amount of value for an unusual amount of people, including those people that engage in Right Livelihood and deliver that value. If you want the wealth, then you should want that responsibility. You should look for problems to solve, be prepared to put in the time and gain the skills to solve those problems, and then build the value delivery process.

## Entrepreneurship and Value Delivery

No one said entrepreneurship and wealth creation would be easy. It is one thing to see a problem that needs solving, but something else to actually see the solution. Even then, some problems are more significant than others, and the solutions more elusive. These are unusual situations, which present the possibility for an unusual amount of value to be given, resulting in that unusual amount of financial reward: wealth. That realization of the solution to those most-perplexing problems is often described as an aha! moment: a sudden realization of an answer or solution, typically represented visually as a light bulb turning on over one's head. I find it appropriate that when Siddhartha, the Buddha, realized the solution to the problems he was seeking to solve, he is described as becoming enlightened. It is said that his aha! moment featured an awakening to the realization of the critical significance of balance – of a middle path. In this case, it was an acknowledgement of the need for appropriate balance in our behaviour. It is this balance that must be considered when contemplating the moral appropriateness of our behaviour in a work environment. We must seek to balance needs – of both those receiving and those providing value.

# 5
# Stakeholders and Leaders

As an organization successfully delivers value, it may start to grow. When it does, the complexity of that organization increases – often considerably. While this is true of businesses, government, and not-for-profit organizations, the reasons for the growth of a business are often related to pursuits of profit, financial success, and wealth creation (at least for the benefit of some). With that growth, ethical issues can become more complicated, more difficult to identify, and certainly more difficult to address. A key factor in this growing complexity is the increasing number of affected parties. A growing business is likely attracting more customers and clients seeking to benefit from the value proposition. Additionally, more people tend to be required in the value delivery process, and more stand to benefit from, or be harmed by, that process. We shall refer to these interested, possibly affected parties as stakeholders.

A stakeholder can be understood as being a person, or a collective of persons (like another company, or the community) that can experience harm, increased unhappiness and even suffering as a result of the product and services provided by an organization, and/or the process that delivers those. Stakeholders are also those people who may experience more happiness or have their suffering reduced as a result of those products, services and processes. Those who engage in a livelihood contribute to the state of happiness or unhappiness experienced by the stakeholders. Right Livelihood refers to those livelihood activities that result in the reduction of suffering and increase in happiness of these stakeholders. Though often acting in concert towards the value delivery objective, various participants in the processes have specific roles that are more likely to impact specific stakeholders. Let's consider some of these roles and stakeholders.

Buddha is a term used to describe an awakened or enlightened person. The expression The Buddha is used to refer to Siddhartha Gautama, upon his storied enlightenment. He is said to have awakened to an understanding, which was to become teachings, and is known as Dharma. These two concepts (Buddha and Dharma) are, together with a third concept, known as the Three Jewels or Three Treasures. The third concept, or treasure, is Sangha. In this context, the word refers to those who are moved by the value proposition of the Dharma and the example of The Buddha. They represent a community of sorts. In fact, Sangha is said to be a word of the Pali and Sanskrit languages which literally means association, community or company. So, a useful way to understand the parable of The Buddha is that, upon his enlightenment, he attracted a company of followers. They were attracted by the opportunity to reduce suffering and increase happiness. This company assisted in communicating this value proposition and sought to exemplify the example set by The Buddha.

This depiction of the initial beginnings of Buddhism is very useful when understanding Right Livelihood. There are three jewels or treasures. Not one or two. They are treated as a collective. As important as a compelling value proposition is, ideas by themselves are unlikely to reduce suffering. As motivating, inspirational and charismatic an entrepreneur, founder or CEO might be, that charisma and enlightened insight alone is unlikely to realize the potential for the increase of happiness. The leader needs a community to form and execute the value delivery process. In the case of a business, that community is made up of employees of various kinds, and they come to represent a very significant class of stakeholder in the success of that enterprise.

To the extent that the members of the organization are actively engaged in the reduction of unhappiness and the increase of happiness that results from the delivery of the value offered, and to the extent that the processes of that delivery do not produce harm, members can be understood as pursuing Right Livelihood. However, it is often hard for the participants to see how they fit into that system – how their livelihood activities result in the intended increase of happiness. This may occur because of the significant distance (in both time and space) between their contribution in the process and the impact on others. They may be engaging in Right Livelihood, but not understand that it is so. Moreover, these participants in the value delivery process are also seeking value themselves. The opportunity to pursue a livelihood is made available by the organization employing them. This is an opportunity to address their own basic needs, such as food and shelter, as well as less basic needs, such as self-esteem and self-actualization. Organizations that are financially successful as a result of delivering value attract employees who see the opportunity to address their own needs and wants by fulfilling the needs and wants of others.

It is the role of management not only to develop and oversee the value delivery process that benefits its customers and clients, but to develop and oversee that which benefits the employees that it seeks to attract and retain. Indeed, employees can be understood to be the clients of management. As such, when managers are engaged in Right Livelihood they are reducing the suffering of, and increasing the happiness of, their clients. There are many ways that such ethical managers can fulfil this responsibility.

For example, a manager engaged in Right Livelihood is ensuring that the processes in place are in fact resulting in the intended value. This may include a wide range of responsibilities depending upon the specific value proposition, including the timeliness of the delivery of the value, and the quality of the product or service intended to produce value. Moreover, this manager engaged in Right Livelihood will be ensuring that employees are contributing to the value delivery process and, importantly, communicating to ensure that the employees can see how they are delivering value. It is essential that management responsibilities include the responsibility to ensure that others recognize how they are reducing suffering and/or increasing happiness, so that they can recognize that they are engaging in Right Livelihood.

Additionally, management roles should include the responsibility to help formulate and deliver the value proposition that is specifically for the employees. To be engaged in Right Livelihood, managers must be addressing the needs and wants of those employees in a manner that results in the reduction of their suffering and the increase of their happiness. Maslow's hierarchy of human needs is relevant again here. Employees have shelter, food and personal safety needs that can be satisfied by sufficient income and safe work environment. From a Buddhist perspective, managers have a moral obligation as part of their livelihood to work to ensure that employees are earning a living wage, being paid entirely for their contribution, and that their work environment is as safe as possible. Employees have needs to feel good about themselves and the work that they do. Managers are obliged to improve the self-esteem of employees, and must certainly refrain from bullying, unconstructive criticism, improper contact, and abusing their power.

To be clear, I am attempting to describe what should be, rather than what many of us are likely to experience consistently throughout our working lives and careers. Unfortunately, many of us will experience toxic work environments or be subject of morally inappropriate conduct from superiors. I have personally witnessed horrific conduct: yelling, berating, bullying, condoning illegal behaviour, physically dangerous work environments, and short-changing staff of earnings. Managers in these environments are sometimes oblivious to the harm, unhappiness, and even suffering that they cause with their behaviour. I imagine that some of these managers, ironically, believe that their behaviour is acceptable – if it seems to deliver more value to the consumer, and more profit to the organization. Yet, these outcomes, if they occur, are short-lived at best. The longevity and sustainability of a value delivery process is required to

## Stakeholders and Leaders

fulfill the potential for value delivery, for staff as well as customers.

The pursuit of Right Livelihood features the objective of reducing suffering and increasing happiness. More of this objective can be achieved if an organization survives successfully to deliver that value. As such, Right Livelihood includes the objective of not merely delivering some value to a customer or client, but to continue to do so over time. The achievement of a long-term sustainable system of value delivery requires a few things to occur. One of these things is that the employees are attracted to the organization by the value that it proposes to provide to both consumers and to themselves. Then they must experience that such value is actually being delivered. When employees (especially those interested in Right Livelihood) come to realize that the organization does not deliver the value to consumers that it purports to do, many may leave… sooner or later. When they come to realize that the value that they are purported to receive (such as compensation, support, acknowledgement, advancement opportunities, appropriate treatment, respect, etc.) is not being delivered, they will most certainly leave… sooner rather than later. Whatever management believes they are gaining (in the short run) by not delivering the proposed value, they will most certainly lose by having employees who do not stay, or do stay, but are not committed to fulfilling their role in the value delivery process.

One of the other requirements for a long-term system of value delivery is the financial viability of that system. Right Livelihood requires managers to ensure the value delivery process is financially sustainable. This includes ensuring that the price of the value is sufficient to (at least) cover the cost of the value delivery. Indeed, the concept of a value proposition includes the price sufficient to generate a product or service that can produce the proposed value, and including the cost of delivery of value to those working in and managing the process.

The costs of the value delivery process includes many costs beyond the cost associated with employees. These include costs related to materials, premises, communications, professional services, and often much more. Those who provide these products and services also stand to receive value or harm by engaging in these processes. They are also stakeholders. They work and live in communities that may benefit from their delivery of that value, and the potential for financial success that may result. So, their community is a stakeholder as well. The largest of companies have employees, processes, procurements, and premises in communities in many parts of the world. Those employers that recognize these stakeholder categories, and actively seek to increase the happiness of these stakeholders, are engaging in Right Livelihood.

In many circumstances, it will be expected that some profit must also be produced, for a system of value delivery to be considered sustainable. Those who receive value because of these profits are also categories of stakeholders. They tend to fall into three groups: 1) government [*by receiving taxes*]; 2) charities [*by receiving donations*]; and 3) investors [*by receiving investment returns*]. These will be considered in more detail in following chapters.

Finally, there is another category of potential stakeholder – though one very often not recognized as such. These stakeholders are the competitors. When an organization successfully executes its value delivery processes, and the value proposition is experienced by its target consumer and customers, as well as other stakeholders, resulting in financial success, competitors will most certainly take notice. They will be eager to offer their own value proposition in an attempt to experience their own financial success, and perhaps even want to experience Right Livelihood from the increase in happiness caused by these efforts. Their value proposition and/or processes for value delivery may be based upon opportunities for differentiation (relative to those of the organization that you may be working in). They maybe be seeing opportunities to differentiate by product, by purpose or by process (as described in the preceding chapter). Competitors may gain some of their success, and especially financial success, at the expense of your organization.

## Stakeholders and Leaders

As such, employees, managers and many other stakeholders may feel threatened by their competitors. They will experience their own goals as competitive: that is, to be successful in their own pursuits, others must be unsuccessful in their pursuits. They will see the competitor's success as somehow resulting in their own failure. As discussed earlier, framing goal environments as competitive in this way establishes the relationship with the competitor in a specific, limited, and often very unhelpful, way. They become an enemy of sorts, and begin to distract from Right Livelihood.

As we learned from the famed Four Minute Mile story, Landy became distracted by the efforts of his competitor, Bannister, and that distraction significantly influenced the outcome of the race. It is critical that an organization not be distracted from the value they are proposing to deliver, the processes that deliver it, and the stakeholders in the process. That is to say, when faced with competition, we must remain focused on the pursuit of Right Livelihood. We must remain focused on reducing suffering and increasing happiness in the manner to which we have committed. Rather, we can benefit by coming to understand our competitors as part of a positive goal environment, with both parties (all parities) benefitting from the success of the other.

This can occur in some very meaningful ways. Competition can motivate each of the parties to improve their value position, and improve their processes; that can result in further problems being solved, for more people, in better ways. In other words, when tackled optimally, competition leads to more Right Livelihood. The organizations involved, and their managers, will also have to improve their value proposition to employees, and the value provided to all the other stakeholders as well. Managers, therefore, are moved by competition to continue to pursue Right Livelihood. When businesses compete in this way, and successes, rewards, and profits are shared, an industry or sector is seen as healthy and vibrant. Consumers, clients, and society at large may come to have confidence in the value positions, beneficial processes, and stakeholder benefits of that industry. This further attracts employees, investment capital, and other business opportunities. Viewed in this light, the relationships among competing organizations and businesses can be seen as positive: the successes of each being realized in a meaningful way by the successes of the other.

Right Livelihood results from the interconnectedness of business organizations, and, as such, competition should be welcomed by those pursuing Right Livelihood. It is the role of the business leader to understand the value proposition of their organization, and their value delivery processes, relative to their competitors. In a very useful way, the existence of a competitor helps the leaders of an organization to come to truly understand what it is, what it should be, what it does, and what it should do. The leaders can come to understand what the organization is by comparing it to a competitor. Its self-identity can result from knowing how it is different from something else. As described earlier in this book, we understand tall because there is something not tall or less tall. The points of differentiation in a value position can emerge for exactly these reasons: to be different from the competitor. As such, the differentiation is more than a description; it can be a prescription. To put it another way, we can choose to compete based on an understanding of what we are in comparison to something else. Then we can change and adjust to be different from that thing or the same as that thing, depending on which outcome is most likely to produce our value delivery objectives.

In this regard, managers are the clients of the leaders, in the sense that leaders provide managers with the direction and resources required to successfully oversee the differentiated value delivery processes. Leaders enable managers to fulfil their Right Livelihood potential. Importantly, leaders must ensure that these adjustments and points of differentiation are communicated to all categories of stakeholders (clients, customers, employees, managers, suppliers, the community at large, etc.) in a way that facilitates their experience of the value. In short, leaders are engaged in Right Livelihood when they are working to adjust and communicate the organization's evolving value proposition to ensure that happiness is increased and suffering is reduced among all categories of stakeholders.

Does this sound like the interconnectedness of various business activities, various responsibilities, and various stakeholder interests can result in some pretty complicated circumstances? Does it sound like it may be hard to know what morally appropriate behaviour is in any given situation, and hard to know if one is truly engaged in Right Livelihood? I hope so, for these are the points I am attempting to make.

The larger an organization becomes, the more participants and stakeholders there are. Larger organizations have the potential to do more harm for more people, and they have the potential to solve more problems, satisfy more needs, and produce more happiness for more people. As such, larger organizations have the potential to generate more financial success for participants. Some may even experience wealth as a result. Indeed, for those wanting to achieve wealth by providing value of increasing significance to increasing numbers and kinds of beneficiaries, creating (or at least participating in) a larger organization is certainly worth considering. Conversely, the possibility of harm resulting from value proposition also means that there is some risk to the participants as well. It has been my experience that when employees, managers, and especially leaders start to lose sight of the organization's value delivery objectives and their stakeholders interests, those risks can start to go up significantly.

One of my own more significant entrepreneurial experiences involved a growing business, with increasing wealth creation potential, and increasing risk. For the first part of my career in the financial services industry, much of the work I had been doing was related to investments and public markets (like mutual funds). I was growing increasingly dissatisfied with the ability of many of those investments to result in the value for which I was hoping. As such, I was also growing increasingly skeptical that I would have my own financial goals satisfied by purchasing such investments. Since I could not see myself selling products that I did not want to purchase myself, I realized I had a problem. Moreover, I knew that others in my industry were likely experiencing the same problem. As an entrepreneur, I recognized this was a problem worth solving, and imagined that if I could find a solution, then significant value could be received and, potentially, by significant numbers. I wanted to engage in Right Livelihood by providing this value, and was hopeful that it would result in befitting financial success. The solution, I felt, might come from participating in private market investments, rather than public market investments.

Knowing my limitations and which skills I lacked, I set upon attracting a business partner. He would become the first member of our Sangha: the first of our growing company of believers in the contemplated value position. Together, we began to attract others. We did this by first clearly understanding how our products and processes were different from our competitors. By knowing those competitors well, I was able to clearly develop and communicate our points of differentiation. Importantly, this was not merely a value proposition for customers; these points of differentiation attracted our employees and managers. They were looking to have their own professional needs met. They were our clients, and we worked to provide the value they were seeking. As a collective, we developed, evolved, and executed our differentiated value delivery processes. This resulted in our initial financial success, which, in turn, attracted more participants and more stakeholders.

As we were building this business, some changes began to unfold. These were regulatory changes that would significantly complicate the value delivery processes we were developing. At first I was quite concerned by the prospect of change, and the unknown implications and impact. Yet, I quickly realized that these changes (implemented by securities regulators) were motivated by a need to benefit and protect consumers. Since this was the same problem we were trying to solve, I embraced the changes, and decided to lead

## Stakeholders and Leaders

our growing team into the unchartered waters ahead. We presented ourselves, and our business, to the securities regulators and became one of the very first companies of its kind in Canada approved to deliver value in the new, regulated environment.

Our desire as an organization to deliver value consistent with the letter and spirit of the regulations began to attract more stakeholders. This interest in Right Livelihood resonated with many. The perception was not only that we could facilitate value delivery effectively, but that, by enthusiastically following the rules, we were reducing specific risks which could harm consumers, and, therefore, harm other stakeholders.

While the relationship between risk and reward was a concept very familiar to me from my many years as an investment advisor, in my new role as an owner of an investment dealership, I was coming to appreciate the significance of that relationship more fully. The financial success that can result from the pursuit of reward does not come without the possibility of not realizing that success. The effort, time, and financial resources that are invested into that pursuit are risked, and a lack of success can result in their loss. This risk is borne, not only by the entrepreneurs, founders and leaders of an enterprise, but by the many stakeholders who are drawn into the endeavours. More than an owner and Director in our business, I had accepted the role of Chief Compliance Officer. This meant that I was responsible for understanding and helping to manage these risks. I embraced this role, and was determined that our organization would set the standard for ethics, compliance and governance in our emerging sector of the financial services industry. My perspective was that, by setting a tone of sincere interest in ethics, we could both increase the likelihood of being successful in our value delivery objectives, and reduce the risk of failure. I believe this approach was critical for what was about to happen.

By my estimation, rising regulatory risks would result in rising costs, and, to address this, we would have to become a bigger organization, delivering more value to more people. As such, I proposed that we seek to merge with a competitor. The candidate was identified and approached. While I knew that our successes would make us attractive, I felt that our commitment to compliance, our ethical reputation, and our risk-managed approach to operations could be a deciding factor. My judgement was confirmed. In a few months a merger was approved and executed, and I found myself to be an owner and Director of Canada's largest Exempt Market Dealership – staying on as Chief Compliance Officer. The value delivery system we had created was now benefitting thousands of stakeholders, including our remaining competitors. However, I had not fully realized my financial reward for my contribution.

One of the benefits of creating a successful business is having someone else want to own it. Before long, another business person wanted to own my stake in the company. I was quite happy to see my efforts come to fruition with a complete exit from ownership and leadership. The process of identifying a problem to solve, through attracting a partner, staff, and a team, engaging regulators and competitors, merging, and (finally) exiting took approximately seven years.

You may find yourself in many different roles, and in many different types of organizations. The various roles will mean that, in the pursuit of Right Livelihood, you will have many different stakeholders for whom to provide value. Here are some the questions you can ask yourself:

Am I ensuring the value delivery system is producing the intended value?

Am I ensuring that employees understand how they are contributing to the value delivery?

Am I encouraging, recognizing, and rewarding that contribution to value delivery?

Am I helping the organization identify the value needed by employees?

Am I helping the organization deliver that value to employees?

Am I considering and addressing the value to other stakeholders, such as suppliers and out-sourced services?

Am I considering and delivering value to the community?

Am I considering and reducing the risk of harm to the community?

Am I working to ensure that the value delivery system is financially viable and sustainable?

Am I providing managers with what they need to bring value to their stakeholders?

Am I providing managers with what they need to reduce the risk of harm to their stakeholders?

Am I leading by example? Am I leading by engaging in Right Livelihood?

Am I helping the organization to understand what it is and what it should be?

Am I engaging competitors in a way that produces mutual benefit and reduces mutual risk?

Am I working to ensure that the business is producing the intended profit?

Am I building a business that someone else would want to own?

I would hope that, in the course of your career and business pursuits, you will have many opportunities to ask many of these questions. Especially, I hope that you will, more often than not, come up with positive and emotionally satisfying answers. "Yes, I am giving value to employees!" "Yes, I am reducing the risk of harm to my community!" But what if you are finding that the answers to some of the questions are negative? This may be your wake-up call and reminder to mindfulness. Take the opportunity to bring your attention and focus mindfully back to your opportunity to bring value to the stakeholders for whom you are responsible. Consider what you can do to change yourself or your processes to improve the value delivery outcomes. If required, approach those in your organization who are responsible to empower you with what you need to complete your role in value delivery. It may be that they are also interested in Right Livelihood, and making their own contribution to value delivery by supporting you.

On the other hand, what if you find that you cannot readily change the causes and conditions resulting in the lack of value? Especially, what if you cannot change the causes of harm, or reduce the risks of harm? What if those around you are not committed to the value delivery processes as perhaps they should be? Especially, what if the leaders of the organization do not seem to be establishing a business culture that emphasizes ethics and compliance? In these cases, you have a more perplexing problem. Mindfully focusing on your specific role and activities will not likely be the best longer term solution. Remember, as you contribute to, and benefit from, processes that do not provide real value, or even produce real harm, you are complicit in those outcomes. Ultimately, you share in the responsibility.

## Stakeholders and Leaders

You may decide to leave and look for the potential to engage in Right Livelihood elsewhere. Or you may decide to stay and influence change. You do not necessarily need to be a leader of an organization to be a leader of change. Theoretically, meaningful change in an organization can be influenced by any role, as each role may contribute to value or harm with different stakeholders and in different ways. Practically, though, matters of ethics are often part of the culture of an organization, and even charismatic and clever leaders may have difficulty adjusting a culture.

An organization's culture is like a person's personality. It forms over time by forces of nurture and nature. The nurture typically comes from founders and leaders, often during the formative years. Nature represents the (often changing) economic, business and regulatory environments that influence how the organization grows and matures. Also like a person, organizations become self-aware. They come to see themselves as distinct from others. Corporations themselves are considered to be legal entities, separate from the individuals who run and own them. Corporations are born, and may die. In a manner of speaking, they are sentient.

According to Buddhist philosophy, all sentient beings have the potential to become awakened or enlightened. This potentiality is sometimes referred to as a Buddha nature. Perhaps it is useful to think of organizations, such as corporations, as having this Buddha nature. An organization can become awakened or enlightened, and you can contribute to this awakening. Like a prince, fully engaged in matters of politics and court behind palace walls, an organization may forget its purpose. Attention must be drawn back to the fact that many are experiencing unhappiness, even to the point of suffering. The organization must have its focus returned to reducing or eliminating the wants and the needs that are the cause of the unhappiness. This is the value it brings to all those stakeholders who benefit, and is the reason for its existence.

This corporate Dharma will need the support of colleagues and other stakeholders: for ideas alone do not cause change. Those compelled by the ideas to act, and encourage others, will form the Sangha: the third jewel of corporate enlightenment.

As described previously, it is said that Siddhartha Gautama's enlightenment featured an appreciation for the importance of balance in behaviour and thinking. Corporate enlightenment must also feature this appreciation. Organizations must come to recognize that their challenge, and opportunity, is to find balance in the delivery of value. The corporation should not be thought of as existing only to provide profit for investors, or enrich founders and leaders. There are a great number of stakeholders to be considered and attended to. There are a great number of people who can be harmed, or receive value from, the products, services and processes of the organization's value delivery. Choosing to find balance in action and thought regarding all such stakeholders exemplifies a commitment to Right Livelihood, and is a true measure of success. In a meaningful way, organizations are not truly separate from these stakeholders. As they benefit, the organization benefits. As they receive value, participants in the organizations will ultimately be rewarded.

# 6
# Communication and Trust

Being able to reduce suffering and increase happiness to one extent or another is the essence of Right Livelihood. To the extent that we can accomplish this – to the extent that we are giving value in balance to various stakeholders – we can achieve financial success. For some, this ability will figure prominently in wealth creation. However, it is not the only ability required.

I have found it extremely useful to think of all business-related and livelihood-related activities as falling into one of two categories:

1. What we do to give value;
2. Communicating about what we do to give value.

Regardless of what you may experience in business school, or training at work, or read in a book about money and wealth, it is useful to think of all behaviour as falling in one of these two categories. To be clear, the skills required to effectively give value and the skills required to communicate about that fact can be very different skills. Moreover, success, and especially financial success, can be far more likely to result from the communication skills over the value delivery skills.

This idea may be counterintuitive for many who begin thinking about, and participating in, business and professional activities for the first time. I believe many of us are influenced by an old expression (attributed to Ralph Waldo Emerson):

"Build a better mousetrap, and the world will beat a path to your door."

This phrase suggests that the means to delivering value and receiving the commensurate financial reward will be found in the quality of the product or service. Further, it suggests that if we can improve on existing products and services, thereby increasing the value that these provide, we may be assured of success.

I believe this notion is simply factually incorrect.

As you may recall from the first chapter of this book, I have a philosophy degree. This included many English courses, and I continued with this study post baccalaureate – thinking that I might teach English if my effort in the financial services industry did not materialize in the ability to support my young family. While I have since dedicated my professional life to education in my field, I have never felt myself to be the brightest or most skilled in my profession, by far. Especially early in my career, I was concerned that my lack of natural abilities would be discovered at some point, and I would fail in my pursuits. Yet, not only did I begin to experience success, but I was quickly becoming more successful than many whom I knew to be better skilled, better educated, and more experienced. Importantly, I came to understand why this was so. I was a better communicator. While others could arguably provide more value, I was better at communicating about the value that I could provide. This led to the actual delivery of value to a greater number of people.

Not only is the better mousetrap aphorism incorrect; it is not useful and perhaps even dangerous. It suggests to the would-be entrepreneur, business person, or anyone engaged in livelihood, that they should be focused entirely on the value and value delivery processes. During my role as Chief Compliance Officer, I interacted with numerous fledgling and experienced entrepreneurs hopeful of raising money to fund a business idea. Since that time, I have continued to coach and mentor such entrepreneurs. I have consistently seen frustration and failure among many, very bright people, who have identified a problem to solve, and a means to give value, but who could not communicate that information in a way that would lead to success. Moreover, I have frequently seen an inverse correlation between value delivery skills and value communication skills among individuals. That is, those who possess problem-solving skills which lead to the experience of some problem solving insight do not also possess the skills to effectively articulate their insight in a way that results in successful value delivery.

So prevalent has this experience been for me, that, in more recent years, I have pursued business opportunities by first identifying those bright people able to deliver value, and helping them communicate that fact to the market, for mutual benefit. I hope that you may find this to be a useful insight in your own pursuits. You may be a person who very much wants to solve problems, deliver value, and achieve wealth, but may be concerned (like I was) that you might not actually have the skills to do so. Communication skills may be the most useful skills of all. Fortunately, these are relatively easy to develop and implement.

I refer to these communications-related activities as a communications strategy. The strategy involves completing five distinct steps. These steps are often, though not always, addressed in this order:

1. Identify the audience(s);
2. Determine response(s);
3. Formulate message(s);
4. Select media;
5. Implement and monitor.

The various audiences are simply those with whom we are communicating. While they may theoretically be individual people, very often they are categories of people. For example, they may be categories of stakeholders: customers, clients, employees, professional services, investors, competitors, members of the community, etc. It is helpful to be able to define or describe each audience category. For example, we may define members of the community as those people who live or work in within a five kilometres radius of a building used by our organization. Further, many categories may be readily divisible into subcategories. For example, an employee may be defined as a person (or entity) that is compensated for their contribution in the value delivery processes of your organization, and be further subcategorized as:

1. **new employee** – one who began to contribute to value delivery within the past three months;
2. **established employee** – one who has been contributing to value delivery for more than three months, but less than one year;
3. **seasoned employee** – one who has been contributing to value for more than one year;
4. **disgruntled employee** – one who has filed a complaint regarding work conditions (regardless of their tenure);
5. **employee on notice** – one who has been warned about their contribution to value delivery.

Of course, there can be many categories and subcategories of audience. The usefulness of how they are defined and categorized is determined by the objectives of the strategy.

For each audience category being addressed, an outcome or response must be determined. This response is the purpose or objective of the communication. Generally speaking, when we communicate, we typically want our audience to receive information (know something), form an opinion (think something), have an emotional responses (feel something), or take action (do something). Yet, it may be hard or impossible to measure that the goals were achieved. These goals are not isolated, but exist together in a holistic complex. One must often infer this achievement or lack of achievement from the behaviour of the audience. For example, suppose that a company initiated a communications strategy with the objective of having the audience of employee have the response of

## Communication and Trust

enjoy their working environment. How would the company know if it was successful? How would it measure an emotion such as enjoy? Perhaps, that emotion could be inferred by how often the employee misses work, or by whether or not the employee introduces the company to friends and family as a place to work. Then the communications strategy should include these measurable behavioural responses.

The message refers to words, images and sounds used in the hopes of achieving the know/think/feel/act, resulting in the measurable behaviour of the target audience. The message(s) may vary as the target audience and the desired responses vary.

The media refers to the methods used to deliver the message(s) to the audience(s): traditional mail, email, social media, TV/radio/print advertising, conversation, print material, posters, and on and on. The media may be dictated by the message. Words themselves can be conveyed in many ways, but sounds and video require specific delivery methods. The choice of media itself can be part of the message. For example, a hand written card expressing thanks to an employee may convey more than a text message of thanks even if the same words are used. The effort we make is often part of the message.

Finally, the communication strategy will include the effort to monitor the responses of the audience(s) to the message(s) to measure whether or not the strategy is successful. If so, repeat. If not, adjust.

This may seem to you to be too simple. I have certainly had marketing professionals tell me as much over my career. Yet, it is the simplicity that makes it useful, and replicable. I have used this very methodology in a wide range of roles, including Director, Board Advisor, committee Chair, business development consultant, recruiter, Marketing Director, and Chief Compliance Officer. Here is an example.

Earlier in my livelihood pursuits, I was a pretty average financial advisor able to provide a pretty average amount of value.

I struggled, as so many do, to deliver more of that value to more people. I came to realize that the most effective, and especially cost-effective, way of finding more of those people was to have potential new clients referred to me. I became very good at executing a communications strategy with that objective in mind. My books, *Awesome Client Events* and *More Awesome Client Events* chronicle the development and results of that strategy.

I had a few different categories of audience in mind. These included some of my best clients, some of my more average clients, and some of the colleagues and other professionals with whom I collaborated. The measurable outcome of the strategy was, first, to have them attend an event with a friend or guest, and, second, introduce me to that friend or guest. Essentially, the measurable outcome was to receive a referral from my target audience at the event. The event itself was a critical part of the message. The audience was invited to attend something fun and interesting. I often selected a novel or unusual venue, and invited adventurous speakers. I made sure that the event was not used to conduct business, but was used to express my gratitude to my clients and colleagues. I made it is clear that I was different from the other financial advisors they might know, and that my clients could expect a different experience. I made it clear that I was very interested in providing what value I could to more people. The delivery of the related messages included printed invitations, tickets, a sincere heart-felt (but brief) speech, as well as pictures and other keepsakes.

This strategy was extremely successful, and was critical in my ability to provide more value to more people, and the financial success that resulted. It also figured prominently in the success of a business I owned (with partners), Canadians Retiring Abroad. With this business, we attracted clients and referring parties by hosting educational events in Mexico. This collaborative enterprise was acknowledged with a coveted Advisor of the Year award in Canada. Even with our strong value proposition, it was not specifically our skills and abilities that garnered that award. It was our ability

## Communication and Trust

to very effectively communicate our abilities – our value proposition and value delivery processes – to the adjudicating bodies that resulted in the response we sought. It is quite conceivable that there were other candidates vying for that award who were in fact more skilled and more enabled to deliver a superior value proposition than we were. Perhaps we were simply better communicators.

This approach to communicating the value proposition and value delivery processes of an organization can be applied to many pursuits. I was invited to provide a workshop to leaders of Buddhist organizations of the Hawaiian Islands on communications strategies, and the very same methodology was enlisted. We first discussed the value proposition of the temples. Then I led the leaders, representing different temples, to identify and clarify the audiences they wanted to address, to determine the specific, measurable responses they hoped for, begin to craft a message, and contemplate what media they might use for delivery.

While you may find yourself engaged in livelihood with a wide range of organizations, with varying value propositions, and differing value delivery systems, this method of developing a system of how to communicate that fact may be the same. Though you may segment your audience into different categories, and look for slightly different responses, prompted by different messages, and through different media, it is likely that you will share at least one objective in common with almost everyone else. One thing that all organizations have in common is the need to establish a degree of trust with their stakeholders.

Trust is required to find capital and financial resources to confirm a solution to a problem. Trust is required to add Human Resources to develop and implement a value delivery system. Trust is required to attract and engage those who will receive value from the systems. Trust is required from regulators, investors, contractors, Directors, and, to some degree, every potential stakeholder. Trust is required from those concerned that they may be harmed by the system. Given the importance of trust, one might think that those involved in such organizations would be particularly knowledgeable of the topic. Yet, most are not.

The approach of a philosopher, when considering an intellectual exercise or debate, is first to define key words or concepts. What is the use, one might reason, of discussing the existence of god without first defining what we mean by that word. I adopt this approach when thinking about trust. Coming to an understanding of a meaning of trust is very useful when beginning to thinking about how to become trusted.

I propose that it is most useful to think of trust as a state of confidence. In this sense, trust is an adjective describing a state of being – that state of confidence – that a subject (the trusting) has in the object (the trusted). It is expressed as "I trust you," or in its negative, "I distrust you." These statements express the existence or lack of confidence. Moreover, I propose that there are two types of confidence.

One of these types of confidence is with respect to the abilities of the object. This is ability trust. It may be expressed as "I trust you are able" or "I trust you can do it." In other words, the object proposes that they can provide value, and the subject comes to trust that they can. The subject has confidence that the object is able to deliver the articulated value proposition – that the professional, or organization, or company, has the skills, processes, staff, resources, etc., to do that which it proposes it can do.

Yet in the fullest sense, the confidence described as trust requires another form. I call this form, integrity trust. This form of confidence may be expressed as "I trust you will do it" or "I trust you have the character or moral disposition to actually do those things that you propose you are able to do." Complete trust of the subject in the object requires that both forms of confidence are present: "I trust you can" and "I trust you will."

The first objective of a communications strategy for all organizations and enterprise is to establish both ability trust and integrity trust. The objective of the strategy is to have the various audiences come to know/think/feel/do, as a response to the message, delivered by the media, and measured by behaviour, that the enterprise has a value proposition, and a system which can successfully deliver that value to the stakeholders. The objective of the strategy is to also have those audiences come to a state of confidence that the value will in fact be delivered as described. Let me emphasize: it is not enough that an organization can provide such value, and will provide such value, it must be seen by the audiences as such. It is the state of confidence that must be established. Success is about much more than building a better mousetrap; it is about being able to communicate that fact. It is about having others come to believe that it is so.

The essence of key Buddhist concepts are often summarized by a subtle, though very useful, communication strategy. Visit a Buddhist temple, and you may see a statue of an exemplar of Buddhist ideals and pursuits with its hands positioned in very specific gestures. Often, each hand is positioned differently. These gestures are known as mudras – representations of how Buddhist philosophy developed the idea that the elimination or reduction of suffering for the practitioner is dependent upon the elimination or reduction of suffering for others. From this perspective, some Buddhists believe that there is an essential pairing of two objectives or ideals: wisdom and compassion. That is: we must strive to have wisdom; we must come to know what to do and how to do it. Simultaneously, we must strive to have compassion; we must care enough about others to put that wisdom to good use. The statues with mudras that represent this idea are communicating the ideal of "I can do it" (ability trust) and "I will do it" (integrity trust).

The most successful in livelihood pursuits are those that can simultaneously communicate to establish both ability trust and integrity trust. When this occurs, they achieve a state of being trusted by the various audiences they are addressing. However, many are able to achieve this state of being trusted without actually being worthy of the confidence they have established. To put it another way, they are not being honest about their abilities to give the value they propose, their commitment to actually delivering that value, or both. They become trusted without being trustworthy. Perhaps they are simply very good at communications strategy. These may be the proverbial unscrupulous salesmen to whom people often refer. While livelihood opportunities and financial success can result from being trusted, Right Livelihood requires both being trusted and being trustworthy. Without being trusted, we will not have the opportunity to increase happiness and reduce suffering. Without being trustworthy, we will not have the ability and/or the integrity to deliver the value when the opportunity arises. As such, the ability to execute communications strategy to establish ability trust and integrity trust is required. This can be much more complicated than merely presenting hand gestures.

Ability trust can be established with an effective communications strategy. As outlined, the process would be to:

1. Identify, list, describe and define the various audiences (and subcategories) that one would like to establish ability trust;
2. Determine the response of the audiences as it relates to know/think/feel/do and measurable behaviour;
3. Craft messages of words, sounds and/or images for the audiences that will result in the responses;
4. Select the media to deliver the messages;
5. Monitor for results, and adjust if necessary.

The messages tend to be the most difficult step of the processes. It might be useful here to think of the message as giving reasons for the trustworthiness of the communicator, and evidence in support of those reasons. For example:

| Reason | Evidence |
|---|---|
| I am trained | Look at my certificate |
| I am educated | Look at my degree |
| I am experienced | See how long I have been doing this |
| I have the tools required | Check out my shop |
| I have the products | Check out my merchandise |
| I have a support network | Here are my affiliates and colleagues |
| I have satisfied clients | Here are some testimonials |
| We have a good reputation | Here are some reviews |

For an individual or for an organization to experience even the most modest levels of successful value delivery, this sort of communication will occur. The stakeholders will come to have confidence, based upon the reasons and the evidence, that the communicator has the skills, abilities and wisdom to do what they propose they can do. The much more challenging part of the communication strategy is crafting and delivering messages that establish integrity trust.

Let's approach this topic, again, as philosophers. If we want to understand how to establish this form of confidence, we should begin by defining our term. Integrity is the sort of word that is used often, especially in the context of business and ethics. Yet it is also a word for which many who employ it do not have a useful definition. In fact, I have seen some pretty unsatisfying definitions in common use. One of my favourites from this category: Integrity means rigorous adherence to the moral rules and duties imposed by honesty and justice. What does this actually mean? How does honesty or justice impose a moral rule? What are these rules? How does this help determine what my behaviour should be? Does this help you know what you should do to establish trust, engage in Right Livelihood, or become wealthy? I have also seen some dangerous definitions. One that is often presented on social media: Integrity is what you do when no one is looking. Not only does this so-called definition not tell me what I should do, it seems to suggest that integrity is somehow private, personal, and not something that needs to be communicated outwardly. It may even be suggesting that those who do communicate about it are making a moral misstep: that talking about having integrity somehow reduces that integrity. As I will argue is a few paragraphs, this can be a very dangerous definition.

While working on one of my professional designations, I was presented with a definition of integrity which I have adopted: Integrity is the alignment of values with action. I have found this to be an extraordinarily useful way of thinking about this concept, especially as it relates to communicating to establish trust. First, it points out that a critical aspect to having and demonstrating integrity is one's behaviour, or the behaviour of an organization. Behaviour is witnessed and experienced. What we do is a form of communication. Our behaviour is an important part of the message we deliver to the various audiences of actual and potential stakeholders, that will lead to know/think/feel/do and measurable responses. That is: establishing integrity trust, the confidence that the communicator will do what they say the can do and will do, will ultimately be based upon our observable behaviour. Yet, our behaviour alone does not establish trustworthiness with respect to integrity. According to my adopted definition, the audience must be able to see that our observable behaviour aligns with our values. How does the audience know what these values are?

The vast majority of the time, the audiences (those current and prospective stakeholders) are not presented with the values of the person or organization engaging them in livelihood. The values are assumed. When you are driving a car along one of Canada's many busy highways, are you concerned that someone will intentionally try to drive their car into your car? Perhaps a little, but not so concerned that you do not drive. Why are we not so concerned? It is assumed that the other driver's values include the importance of their own personal health and well-being, the value to them of keeping their vehicle in good working order, and respect for the value of health of the passengers in their vehicle and in other vehicles. We assume that their values include how they spend their time, and respect for how you want to spend your time as well; they would much rather get to where they are going, rather than stop to deal with an accident, or take the time to fill reports, make insurance claims, get their car fixed, etc. We assume that their values include their personal freedom (and, so, do not want to be incarcerated). For our society to function in this way, there must be a minimum level of ability trust and integrity trust. We must trust that they have the basic skills to drive and a vehicle in reasonable operational condition. The evidence for this trust may be an expectation that they have passed a driver's exam and are legally permitted to operate a vehicle. We must also trust that they will choose to drive appropriately: which means (in this context) in a way that demonstrates the assumed, shared values. This state of shared trust and assumption of shared values makes for a workable social environment most of the time.

When a person or an organization is communicating to establish integrity trust, they may choose to rely solely on an assumption of shared values. For example, in the course of fulfilling a livelihood activity, you might schedule an appointment or commit to completing work in a certain way, by a specific date and time. Your behaviour (being on time for the appointment or completing the work) is experienced by the audience, who might infer that this behaviour aligns with your values (which they assume), and might, therefore, be evidence that you have integrity. However, one of the easiest and most effective ways to improve this aspect of communications strategy is to actually communicate those values. This can be done somewhat informally. You may say:

"I will be on time and ready for our appointment at 10:00 am. You will find that I am always on time and ready as promised. It is important to me that I demonstrate to you that you are important and your time is valuable. The first way I will demonstrate my respect for you will be by being on time."

Or, within the context of a communication strategy:

- **Audience**: prospective client
- **Purpose**: establish integrity trust, establish confidence that the communicator will do what they say they will do
- **Message**: "I will be on time and ready..."
- **Media**: delivered by voice, phone conversation

When an organization communicates to establish integrity trust, it may benefit from a more formal approach. For example, drafting a values statement. An organization's objective may be expressed by a mission statement and stated goals. These ideas will convey what it is attempting to do and perhaps how it intends to do it. However, a values statement will communicate why it wants to do these things, or why these things are worth doing. Behaviour is motivated by values, and the audience may gain some confidence that the organization will do that which it proposes it will do by the message of why it finds such behaviour to be important.

- **Audience(s)**: prospects, clients, staff, management
- **Purpose**: establish integrity trust, establish confidence that the communicator will do what they say they will do
- **Message**: "Here is our statement of values: We believe that everyone is worthy of respect. We believe that the first way we can show respect is by being on time and ready for every meeting. We believe that the second way we show respect is by completing our work as promised. We believe that the third way we show respect is by providing all members of our team with what they need to be on time, be ready, and complete their work as promised."
- **Media**: stated on website, stated on client-facing brochures, stated on a poster displayed in staff room, stated verbally at the beginning of monthly staff meetings

This values statement can help the audience understand that the behaviour they experience is in alignment with the values of the organization, demonstrating integrity, and being evidence for the establishment of integrity trust. It communicates that the organization has enough compassion for the audiences (clients, staff, management, etc.), that it will fulfill its commitment of the delivery of its wisdom (value).

The other message being conveyed by a values statement is the idea that communicating about values is important. It is not just that the organization has values, but that its members accept that sharing values is a meaningful part of livelihood pursuits, and that being trustworthy is important.

Moreover, I propose, that Right Livelihood includes the sharing of values in this way. Since integrity is an alignment of values with action, and stating values can contribute significantly to this perception (as opposed to assuming specific values are present), the ability to communicate values within a communications strategy is essential for demonstrating trustworthiness. Being trustworthy, and communicating that fact, increases the likelihood of being trusted, which increases the likelihood of delivering the value proposition, which increases the likelihood of increasing happiness and reducing suffering. The effective pursuit of Right Livelihood, therefore, requires more than having values, or having specific values; it requires being able to communicate about that fact.

I have found that another, potentially significant, benefit of sharing values as part of livelihood activities: it encourages the audience to communicate their values back. This was especially useful when I was working as a financial advisor. Typically, my clients, as with almost everyone else, had a fairly limited amount of financial resources. How they would apply those resources to specific objectives would be a reflection of their values. They would prioritize how they would spend, save or invest the money they received based upon what was more or less important to them. By coming to understand their values, I could better understand their priorities. In some cases, this would help me decide that they would not be the type of client I was seeking. In other cases, it would help me determine which financial strategies or products would appeal to them the most.

With my Canadians Retiring Abroad business, I conducted research on the demographics of those I thought might be a target audience for our firm's retirement services. Michael Adams, one of Canada's best-known demographers, has written extensively on sub-categories of Canadians. He divides adult Canadian key demographic categories (like baby boomers) into sub-category psychographic cohorts based upon shared values of each group. By understanding how these groups differed by values, I was better enabled to determine who might be more likely to find an international retirement experience enticing, and, therefore, maybe more likely to benefit from the services we provided.

Another fairly common, formal method for encouraging trustworthiness is a code of ethics or statement of professional responsibility. These somewhat more complex and lengthy messages are typically delivered primarily to an audience of those whose behaviour it is hoped will be influenced. Such audiences are often professionals, association members, or designation holders. I have been reviewing, drafting, and teaching such codes for the financial services industry for many years. It is debatable as to how effective such codes are in terms of influencing behaviour, and, therefore, in terms of their usefulness towards improving integrity. The audience's values may not also include the importance of such codes, or the importance of the ideas expressed by such codes. However, I have certainly concluded that such codes are typically very ineffective as a tool for establishing trust. This is for the simple reason that such codes are typically not effectively communicated to other audiences with whom those professionals, association members, or designation holders, whose confidence the message senders are hoping to gain.

Drafting a code of ethics and not sharing the code with other audiences is a missed opportunity to provide evidence in support of integrity trust. Communicating that such a code exists, and especially about the behaviour meant to be influenced by that code, provides a message to various stakeholder audiences about the values of the communicator. This communication can help an audience know values, and, therefore, makes possible a determination of the existence of integrity.

One of the services I have provided to financial advisors is completing an ethics audit. This audit was meant to review the processes of the advisor, to provide an objective means of measuring those processes from an ethics perspective. While the advisor may gain some insight on how to make some improvement in these processes, most of the advisors that sought out, and paid for, such services, already had a pretty good sense that the audit would be somewhat favourable. Indeed, that is why they wanted the audit: so they could have a report created by an objective, knowledgeable third-party. The report could serve in a communications strategy as evidence in support of integrity trust.

In more recent years, I have been serving as a Director on the boards of public and private companies, acting as an advisor to such boards, or serving on committees (often the Investment Review Committee). From these roles, the contribution to ensuring integrity within the organization, and contributing to communication strategy to confirm trustworthiness that leads to the establishment of trust, can include a variety of behaviours. Some of these are related to governance, where the values assumed of, or stated by, the leaders are measured against their behaviour. For example, a message that whistle blowing is permitted and encouraged (as a value) would be measured against the existence of whistle blowing policies and procedures, and the actual response of a Director or Board to an incident of whistle blowing. A board that purports to embrace the value of informed decision-making, for example, can be measured against the clarity, transparency, timeliness, and completeness of its communications to its various stakeholder audiences. Even in their personal lives, their behaviour will expose their true values and motivations. They will lead by example, whether that example contributes to value delivery and exemplifies Right Livelihood, or does not. These behaviours and values set the proverbial tone from the top, and are critical in the establishment of integrity trust.

In my role as Chief Compliance Officer and owner of an investment dealership, I was known for espousing a simple but very useful mantra: It is not enough that we do the right thing, was must be seen as doing the right thing. More than a tone from the top, this was a battle cry. I recognized that doing the right thing, behaving morally and legally, behaving in a manner that aligned with our values, was not simply a matter of doing good, it was a matter of doing good business. Being seen as doing the right thing would attract customers, staff, management, and other stakeholders, by our values, to our value proposition and value delivery processes. This would lead to revenue opportunities. Being seen as doing the right thing would also help reduce risks of various kinds: regulatory, reputational, legal, third-party, and more. I believed that this approach helped with our initial success, and may even have encouraged our competitors to adopt a similar corporate philosophy. A good business seeks that balance between reward and risk. A good business is something that someone else will want to own. Selling that business to that someone else can result in financial success, and even wealth.

In this way, Right Livelihood that leads to wealth creation is a matter of both value delivery and communicating about value delivery. It is a matter of first being trustworthy and then being trusted. Optimally, it is the objective to have stakeholders of all kinds arrive at a state of confidence in both abilities and integrity of the organization and its leaders. If you are engaged in Right Livelihood, wise enough and compassionate enough to increase happiness and reduce suffering, and, therefore, worthy of the trust you seek to establish with your market, you have an obligation to communicate that fact. This obligation arises, in part, from the fact that there are others out there who are establishing trust with the market, but are not actually trustworthy. These may be criminals, or merely the incompetent, the inept, or the unwilling. If they are

## Communication and Trust

the only ones saying, "Trust me! I can be trusted! I am worthy of your trust!" then they will gain the ear of stakeholders, but value delivery will not result. Not only will happiness not increase, but actual suffering may increase. You have an obligation to communicate your trustworthiness more effectively, with more conviction, and more evidence, to entice stakeholders to your value delivery so that true value will be experienced. Integrity is not about what you do when no one is looking; it is about doing your best to make everyone look.

# 7
# Spending Mindfully

For those who engage in Right Livelihood, become trustworthy, and communicate to establish trust, there will be many opportunities to solve the problems of, and give value to, many stakeholders. As these stakeholders benefit from reduced suffering or increased happiness, those providers of value will receive value themselves.

An important part of this value, and possibly a significant motivator for behaviour, is the financial reward that typically accompanies such value delivery. Those engaged in Right Livelihood are poised to have their personal, financial goals realized, perhaps even to the point of achieving wealth.

So what? So what's next?

The financial reward received is not the end of Right Livelihood. Money received is not stagnant. By definition, all money received is either spent or saved. There are ramifications, responsibilities, and opportunities in either case. Financial resources are causes and conditions that lead to other sates of affairs. Let's start by considering spending from a Right Livelihood – from a Buddhist – perspective.

Some may associate Buddhism or Buddhist ideals with austerity. They may be influenced by images they have seen of humble monks, who have given up their possessions, living in a simple and plain way, with little or no money, and perhaps even surviving on the generosity of others. The story of the Buddha, leaving the palace and princely comforts, and living ascetically, may encourage this perspective. However, his storied awakening or enlightenment ultimately featured the realization of the importance of balance, and not of strict self-denial. The begging monk can be better understood, not as a person who idealizes dependency on others, but as a person who is giving another person the opportunity to be generous. That monk can be seen as providing the opportunity for another to give value, and even for providing the opportunity for that other to engage in Right Livelihood.

I propose that the best way to understand Right Livelihood, within our contemporary context, includes giving others the opportunity to engage in Right Livelihood themselves. As it is morally appropriate, even obligatory, for us to use our wisdom, skills, and experience, within the value delivery processes we participate, to compassionately reduce suffering and increase happiness, it must be so for others. For those others, engaging in Right Livelihood will require willing participants, interested in having their own problems solved and needs addressed. As we receive financial reward from our own Right Livelihood, we have the obligation to help others engage in theirs.

We can do this by spending, aware of our connectedness. We can spend with gratitude. I am grateful that I have the wisdom and the compassion to provide value to others, and that those others are willing to participate in my value delivery process. I am grateful that I receive financial reward for my contribution. I am also grateful that others have the wisdom and compassion to solve my problems and address my needs. I am grateful to have the financial resources to reward them for making my life better. I am grateful for this interdependency.

Not all spending will qualify as participation in Right Livelihood. We must spend mindfully. That is, when spending, we must consider whether or not suffering is truly being reduced, or happiness is truly being increased. Those considerations, that may help us understand the appropriateness of livelihood pursuits, may also help us understand the appropriateness of our spending behaviour. There are three primary categories of spending: consumption (products and services), tax, and charity.

## Spending Mindfully

When considering spending money on a product or service, we should begin with the following questions:

- Will this product or service harm me?
- Will it harm me almost certainly?
- Will it harm me just possibly?
- What is the value that is being proposed to me?
- Is it a means value or an ends value?

How is it proposed that this product or service will address my needs, solve my problems, reduce my suffering, or increase my happiness?

I propose that our Right Livelihood activities include spending our money on products and services that, first, do not harm us when those products and services are used as intended. In my opinion, cigarettes cause harm when used as intended. Right Livelihood does not include spending money on cigarettes.

There are other products that may increase suffering and reduce happiness, or they may reduce suffering and increase happiness. The outcome depends upon how they are used. These might include products such as alcohol, firearms, and motor vehicles. These might include gambling services. Purchasing such products and services have the potential to contribute to Right Livelihood, but could easily cause suffering as well. Since, to be engaged in Right Livelihood, the providers of such products and services should ensure that their efforts are resulting in value delivery, rather than harm delivery, their efforts must include processes encouraging that outcome. Right Livelihood for them requires education, controls, and other forms of mitigation to reduce or eliminate the outcome of harm. Some products and services may have the potential to increase happiness only if the product and service provider is trustworthy. Investment products and services may fall into this category. As such, spending mindfully should include asking additional questions:

- Is the proposed value of the product and service really a value?
- Will I, personally, experience a reduction of suffering or increase in happiness if I spend money on this product or service?
- Is the provider of the product or service trustworthy?
- Do I have the confidence that they have the ability to deliver the proposed product or service in a way that results in the intended value?
- Do I have the confidence that they have the integrity to deliver the product and service as promised?

As prospective consumers, we are the targets of communication strategy. Communicators have identified us as an audience, and are intending to have us know, think, feel, or do something in a way that can be measured by our behaviour. They hope that this behaviour will feature spending our money. They are crafting and delivering messages to accomplish this objective. Spending mindfully includes being aware of these communications strategies. We may be receiving messages, arriving at states of confidence, and experiencing trust, even when the communicators are not worthy of that trust. We should be mindful of these communications, and ask:

- Am I being provided with real evidence in support of the ability trust the communicator is attempting to establish?
- What am I thinking (as it relates to trustworthiness) because of these communications?
- What do I now know and how does this support ability trust?

Just as we would present our skills, education, experience, and support systems, as evidence that we could deliver the value we propose in the course of our livelihood, we should expect that such evidence is provided to us by others. This is not merely for our own protection. By ensuring (as best as we can) that the communicator is worthy of the ability trust they seek – that they can actually

## Spending Mindfully

deliver the proposed value – we are doing our part in ensuring that the communicator is engaging in Right Livelihood. Since engaging in Right Livelihood reduces suffering and increases happiness for the provider of that value as well as the receiver, we are benefitting all parties when we are spending mindfully.

Similarly, spending mindfully includes looking for evidence in support of the integrity trust that the communicator is attempting to establish:

- Why should I believe that this person or company will do what they say they will do?
- Am I being presented with evidence of their values?
- Are these values consistent with my own?
- Are these values likely to produce the behaviour I am looking for?
- Am I being presented with confirmation that the person or company subscribes to a code of conduct or code of ethics?
- Do I have reason to believe that such codes would influence behaviour, resulting in integrity?
- Is there evidence that the leadership of the organization has integrity?
- Am I aware of leadership behaviour and values?
- Is there evidence that leadership attracts, acknowledges, and rewards stakeholders for doing the right thing?
- Am I truly seeing the behaviour, and all of the behaviour, so that I can adequately measure for an alignment with the values?

As a business person, I am particularly interested in evidence as a precursor to a state of trust. I recognize that one might arrive at a state of confidence in a person or an organization's ability and integrity and not be really sure as to why that has happened. We may have been the object of a communication strategy that does not overtly and clearly communicate evidence. Indeed, we may not readily perceive in any of the messages something specific that includes information that leads us to know something, or come to think something, that justifies the confidence we are experiencing. The messages are producing the intended confidence, and possibly the intended behaviour, based on feeling only. From a Right Livelihood perspective, I am extremely skeptical about such communications strategies.

When I experience marketing, branding, sales processes, and other communications, that are very heavy on feeling and emotions, and very light on evidence, I become suspicious that there is not really a value to the product and service being offered. I challenge the notion that a feeling by itself should be considered representative of the reduction of suffering and the increase of happiness. I propose that it is more useful to think that a feeling may accompany that reduction or increase, but is not the value *per se*. I have this sentiment when, for example, I consider the value of something like soft drinks. These sorts of products are often presented with images and sounds like music or laughter, that I believe are designed to have prospective consumers experience specific feelings. It is not my intent to have you conclude there is no real value available to you by purchasing such a product. I merely invite you to consider what that value really is. If you purchase such products, do so mindfully, and assure you are engaging in Right Livelihood.

A related concept is what I call the emotional premium. This refers to the portion of the product or service that does not provide a true value to the consumer. The value proposition offered by a person or business includes the cost of that product or service. Some of that cost is attributable to the processes required to create and deliver that value. Sometimes, however, there can be a portion of the cost of a solution to a problem or the addressing of a need that may have little to do with that problem or need. For example, we may consider a need to have clothes. Clothes provide protection from the elements and can contribute to physical survival. A shirt can be seen as providing this sort of value. A shirt that is clean, without rips and holes, that fits reasonably well, that does not offend others, might also be seen as a need. We need to present ourselves reasonably and with a certain amount of decorum, to be accepted by others and to function in a way considered to be normal in many societies.

Moreover, one may even argue that some will have a need for a nice shirt, pressed, and collared, to have the confidence to engage effectively in many Right Livelihood activities. Whether you think this should be true or not is immaterial (pun intended). A shirt to address the need of basic survival might be recoverable from a garbage bin at little or no cost. A shirt to address the need of fitting in to many social circumstances might be purchased from a second hand store, or most basic clothing retail distribution systems for a fairly modest cost. A nice dress shirt, considered business attire and appropriate for many work environments, and able to address the needs of self-actualization, may be purchased for a little bit more money. However, what of those who purchase clothes that cost much, much more? While they may argue that it helps them to feel good about themselves and confident, even superior to others, should this be considered as a real value? Should this be considered as truly reducing suffering and increasing happiness in the spirit of the expression? I suggest that when such persons are spending this way, they are addressing a need, but also paying an emotional premium. Perhaps it is the logo on the shirt that is adding to this cost. The logo, as an aspect of the message of the communications strategy, is designed to have the audience experience a feeling that may lead to behaviour. This feeling is what the emotional premium is paying for. A consumer, when spending mindfully, will recognize how their spending is actually resulting in Right Livelihood, and how their spending is merely covering the cost of the emotional premium.

We can apply this perspective to a host of products and services on which we might spend money. When contemplating an outfit, a decoration, a car, a house, a dinner out, a haircut, spending mindfully will include such questions as:

- How much of the cost of the product or service is really about fixing a problem or addressing a need?
- How much of the cost of this product is really about my desire to feel superior, to parade my financial success or wealth?
- Is my spending rewarding a provider of a product or service for engaging in livelihood activities that do not actually reduce suffering and increase happiness?
- Am I paying for branding that does not meaningfully contribute to the value?
- Am I simply buying a feeling?

Personally, when it comes to purchases that might be associated with evidence of financial success, I have tended to own homes and vehicles of fairly average costs. I have tended to be motivated by the real value I would receive from such purchases, rather than how my circumstances might appear to others. Having had the opportunity over 30 years to review detailed, self-reported, financial circumstances of literally hundreds of Canadians who would be considered to be of average to affluent means, I can tell you with confidence that many do not take this approach. Many are moved to present themselves, by their homes and cars, as having more financial means than they do. This seems to be particularly true of many young professionals and sales persons I have encountered, who are guided by the mantra: fake it until you make it. Or, as I would clarify:

"Misrepresent your level of success to your prospective market, in the hopes that they may infer the existence of ability and integrity, until you actually have such ability and integrity that would produce the delivery of such value to such numbers, resulting in the financial reward associated with your representation."

On the other hand, I have tended to spend more money on three types of services: education, health (exercise) and travel. This behaviour reflects my values: that experiences resulting in personal growth and betterment yield more real value for me than buying stuff. I am not suggesting that you adopt such values, or such behaviour. I am inviting you be mindful of your own values, your motivations, and how these values become manifest in your spending. I invite you to ask: what value am I actually receiving when I consume?

The second line of inquiry that we should pursue when spending on products and services is with respect to the processes that result in those products and services. While we may receive value ourselves from these, we should also wonder how these processes create experiences for other stakeholders. As discussed, the attempt to deliver value to consumers requires processes that can involve a great number of stakeholders, including staff, suppliers, community members, investors, and even the environment. Questions we should ask include:

- Is someone being harmed by the processes used to bring this value to me?
- Is a community being harmed by these processes?
- Is the environment being harmed by these processes?
- Are these processes bringing value to persons other than myself? If so, how?
- Are these processes bringing value to a community, or improving the environment?

Spending mindfully includes a consideration for how value is received, or harm created, on balance to various stakeholders. It is a continuation of the Right Livelihood activities that provides the financial resources we require to consume. I am most grateful when I am aware that my spending is not only resulting in my own reduction of suffering and increase of happiness, but when I am also aware that this behaviour is reducing the suffering and increasing the happiness of others.

Practically speaking, we must consume, to some extent, to

have our needs addressed in modern society. Many needs, however, are also addressed by spending that is not on products and services as a consumer. An important category of this type of spending is in the form of taxes that we pay. Taxes can arise for a variety of reasons: based upon products and services we buy, or the income we earn from our livelihood pursuits, or perhaps from business or investment activities. It is proposed by those who establish policies and procedures (like governments) that result in the payment of taxes, that we, the taxpayers, will receive value from these processes. This value might be in the form of a system that provides education or health care, or services related to policing and defence, or the creation and maintenance of transportation infrastructure, or to enabling and stimulating an economic and business environment. These provide benefit in varying degrees to members of society, and also may provide the opportunity for those whose employment and business activities arise from these to engage in Right Livelihood.

On the other hand, government bodies attempting to provide such services may not in fact have the ability or the integrity to deliver the proposed value to which they have committed. Representatives of government bodies that communicate in the hopes of establishing a state of confidence in the taxpayer, may be representing processes that may not be trustworthy…at least not to the degree that would satisfy their audience. Government-organized solutions to problems are often criticized as not being the most effective or efficient means to the desired ends. Nevertheless, judging from the relative lack of suffering in my own country and the relative state of happiness enjoyed by many, it certainly seems that the value delivery processes are working reasonably well. What might we conclude about tax-paying as it relates to spending and Right Livelihood?

I propose that Right Livelihood behaviour should include paying taxes as required by law, but not a nickel more. Tax evasion occurs when a tax payer is not paying taxes as required by law. I reason that, since we benefit from the systems and processes that rely on taxation, Right Livelihood requires that we contribute financially to such systems and processes. In a meaningful way, our ability to attain the skills and abilities to deliver value, and the ability of our proposed willing participants to pay us for these, depends upon those systems and processes around us. We should mindfully, and (as much as we can muster) gratefully, become aware of the value we receive from the payment of these taxes. We should not engage in tax evasion.

However, it is also important that we recognize that other types of organizations, such as for-profit and not-for-profit non-government organizations may also be able to provide solutions to these problems. It may also be that these other organizations are better enabled to bring more value, and perhaps even at a lower cost. It is critical that we have not only the ability to exercise choice as we spend in the pursuit of value, but that we actually exercise that choice. By paying the minimum amount of tax required, we are able to exercise our choice and allocate those financial resources in a manner that provides the greatest amount of value, with the least amount of harm. Tax avoidance refers to the legal means available to taxpayers to reduce the amount of taxes they pay. Various incentives and rules are provided that permit this avoidance, though assistance in pursuing and applying these is often required. As such, I also propose that, if Right Livelihood includes the payment of the minimum amount of tax required, then those engaged in Right Livelihood also have an obligation to seek out those services that will help them lawfully reduce those taxes. Not only is this an expression of Right Livelihood, it is perhaps the second most important factor (after value delivery) contributing to the morally appropriate achievement and maintenance of wealth.

I propose that, in the course of spending mindfully on tax, we should ask:

- Are the taxes I am paying providing me with value? How?
- Are the taxes I am paying enabling others to engage in

Right Livelihood by reducing my suffering or increasing my happiness?
- Are these taxes enabling the creation of harm?
- Are there other, non-government organizations that are/could addresses these needs more effectively and efficiently?
- Am I paying the appropriate amount of tax to fund the system and processes?
- Could I lawfully reduce my taxes and redeploy those financial resources to other value delivery systems?
- What services do I require to know the answers to these questions?

The third category of spending available to us is in the form of charity. Unlike spending as a consumer on products and services, or as a taxpayer on taxes, we typically have more control and choice regarding the allocation of financial resources to charities, and other forms of not-for-profit organizations. The value proposition of many of these types of organizations focuses on the value that might be received by parties other than those providing the financial resources and those providing the value delivery processes.

We are invited, primarily, to provide funds so that value is received by someone or something other than ourselves. Those communicating to us in the hopes that we provide such funds tend to offer a message that is more about having us come to feel something, rather than think or know something. It may not be clear from the communications strategy the extent to which those other parties are actually benefitting from the value delivery processes. Indeed, we may not come to know from meaningful evidence for sure to what extent, if any, those proposed beneficiaries are actually experiencing a reduction of suffering or an increase in happiness. Instead, we are communicated to with the desired response of having us feel something, like sadness and empathy arising from the suffering of others, or like guilt for the happiness we are experiencing and the financial resources we have. It seems to me that a value that some charities and similar organizations are really proposing to deliver is having us, the prospective contributor, feel better about ourselves. As already expressed, I do not recognize a feeling *per se* as a real value received.

Charitable organizations may benefit, as other forms of organizations, from increasing size and growing resources. However, such growing organizations may also suffer from declining confidence (and, therefore, declining trust) among its contributor stakeholders. In other words, the size and distance between the contribution of funds and the proposed value to the proposed beneficiaries may be so great that it becomes difficult, or impossible, to know if the value position is being fulfilled. In modern society, the decision to support a charity, and the potential ramifications of that choice, will be significantly different from the immediacy of providing a monk with a bowl of rice. We must ask:

- Is this charity actually providing value to the beneficiaries?
- What is the evidence for this?
- Is the charity merely communicating to have me feel something?
- Does the charity have the ability to deliver the value to the beneficiaries as proposed?
- Does the charity have the integrity to do as it reports it will do?
- What is the evidence in support of integrity trust? Values statements? Codes of ethics? Third-party audits?
- Who or what is ultimately receiving the value from the financial resources provided by contributors?

To be clear, I am not suggesting that there is not merit to the work of charities. I am not suggesting that those working there are not engaged in Right Livelihood, or that a contribution from you would not be in furtherance of your own Right Livelihood. However, I am certainly advocating for mindfulness when contemplating spending in this way. Some charities actually allocate a very small amount of the funds raised to produce the value proposed to the prospective beneficiaries or cause. There are some charities that compensate staff, managers and leaders in amounts that would seem to be disproportionate to the amount of real value caused by those persons. Moreover, it seems to me that, at least in some cases, people are achieving personal wealth, though not from providing an unusual amount of value to an unusual number of persons. If we are supporting and enabling such behaviour by our spending, then we are complicit in the outcomes. It should not be assumed that by supporting a charity, we are automatically acting in furtherance of our own Right Livelihood.

To better understand the potential for value creation that may result from financial support to a charity or not-for-profit organization, the prospective supporter may want to do some research. They may want to better understand who or what will actually receive value from a donation. Financial statements are often made available to the public, containing valuable information on how revenues (like donations) are spent. Such statements, however, may be hard to decipher for those who may be inclined to contribute. This is a problem that some entrepreneurs are attempting to address by offering services that conduct assessments and provide ratings of charities. The objective is to provide value to would-be donators by providing clear, objective information that might enable them to arrive at a state of confidence in the ability and the integrity of that charity, or not. I suggest that Right Livelihood does not require supporting charities or not-for-profits, but, for those moved to apply their funds in this way, Right Livelihood does require that such research occur first.

After conducting some research on how not-for-profits actually spend the money they receive, and who or what, specifically, is receiving value, you may come to feel disheartened. I know I have had such feelings. I might be described as naturally skeptical of the true motivations of persons who profess to be seeking financial

## Spending Mindfully

support, not for themselves, but for value delivery to others. Fortunately, we have the means to organize our own not-for-profit endeavours, and create value delivery systems that reflect our values and our expectations. Our family, for example, decided to establish the Foundation for the Advancement of Entrepreneurship (www.fae.ngo). We were looking for a way to spend mindfully, and hoping to be able to assist with solving a problem. However, we quickly recognized that there are a great number of problems to solve and people needing help. We could not decide which problem to focus on. How could we choose to help one person over another? Consequently, we decided that what we actually needed was more, and better, problem solvers. Perhaps with more skilled and committed problem solvers, more problems could be addressed, resulting in more happiness created. As such, we decided that our foundation would promote such entrepreneurial and financial skills, and the associated mindset, among young adults. We decided that we would do this by providing post-secondary scholarships to students who pursue entrepreneurial education, and who can describe how entrepreneurship improves their community. Also, we wanted to ensure that the foundation was running efficiently and effectively, so that funds received could result in as much of this value as possible. We are fortunate in that we have collaborated over the years with a variety of successful, like-minded business persons and professionals – many of whom have been happy to assist with the foundation's efforts. In addition to donating my time as Director, I have been using proceeds from speaking and writing to help provide funds. Indeed, if you purchased this book, you are likely contributing to these scholarships.

As we spend our money on products, services, taxes and charities, we are offering a form of support to those organizations. To the extent that such organizations are truly reducing suffering and increasing happiness, our support may be seen as an extension of our own Right Livelihood. Conversely, to the extent that such organizations are not providing processes that result in value, or, worse, have processes that result in harm, we are complicit in those outcomes as well. Fortunately, we often have a choice, and sometimes considerable choice, as to whom or what we support with our hard-earned funds. As mindful spenders, we can potentially use our funds to influence the behaviour of these organizations. By withholding our money, and choosing not to support a particular business, product, service, or charity, we may have the ability to encourage an improvement of the proposed value proposition and value delivery processes.

This form of consumer activism has been popular for many years. I have enjoyed many conversations with (often younger) consumers about how they purchase or do not purchase, or where they shop or will not shop, based upon their values and the processes of various businesses. I ask them:

How does this influence the behaviour of those businesses?

In most cases, they do not know. Nor could they. Simply choosing to not support a business and their processes, by not engaging financially, will not likely be the most effective influence for change. Through our spending, we have the ability to bring value to these processes. Yet, as I argued in the previous chapter, the ability to bring value is typically not the most important contributor to the reduction of suffering or the increase of happiness. The most significant factor is often the ability to communicate. As such, I propose that effective consumer activism will include a communications strategy, in addition to supporting or withholding support, financially. Consumers who want to increase the likelihood of change, specifically in their role as consumers, are advised to:

1. Identify the various audiences (like business, government, charity);
2. Determine the measurable responses in behaviour of the audience;
3. Craft the message(s) – more than their behaviour as a consumer;

## Spending Mindfully

4. Select the media for the delivery of the message.

For example, let's suppose that you disapprove of an organization or perhaps you disapprove of the behaviour of it leaders. You could choose to not spend money on its products and services. If these are offered through a retail distribution channel, like on-line or a store at your local mall, you may also choose to avoid those channels entirely. However, your absence from their value delivery processes may go entirely unnoticed. You are one of perhaps millions of customers, and the fact that you did not buy something recently may not be a significant point of information. On the other hand, a communication strategy that includes letting those manufactures and distributors know that you are not participating financially, and why you have made that decision, may be more likely to result in the behaviour you are hoping for from them.

Spending mindfully as an extension of Right Livelihood includes both being aware of our spending, and the influences and conditions that arise from that spending. It is also about recognizing that spending, as a form of behaviour, becomes an aspect of how we communicate. Optimally, it can be seen as a feature of a communication strategy that may increase happiness and reduce suffering. However, spending, as an activity in itself, however mindful, does not typically lead to wealth creation for the spender. While our spending may lead to wealth creation for those receiving our money, and, hopefully, providing us with value, we are more likely to experience our own wealth creation when spending modestly.

Since, by definition, all the money we receive is either spent or saved, money not spent is, therefore, saved. By spending modestly, and only seeking the real value available to us as a consumer, taxpayer and contributor to charity, we can have savings left for other purposes. These savings are, by definition, part of the capital markets – in some form or another. These savings can be understood as the potential for future spending, and so, for future contribution to value delivery processes. However, even in the form of savings, they are also contributing to value delivery processes. It can be further reasoned that, since our saved financial resources are more likely to result in more money in the future than those funds spent, saving has the potential to ultimately create more value than spending. Let's consider how saving and investing mindfully can result in greater value creation, and wealth.

# 8
# Investing Mindfully

There are many ways that we can contribute meaningfully to a value delivery process, and, as such, many activities that can be associated with Right Livelihood. How we conduct ourselves when we earn our living and how we conduct ourselves when we spend what we earn are two of these. Yet, if we do not spend all that we earn, we begin to create the possibility for the third way to contribute meaningfully. This third way is as an investor.

Savings are defined as that which is not spent, and all savings exist in some way in a financial system known as the capital markets. This system includes hard currency (even if it is in your wallet or purse, or hidden under your mattress) as well as funds you have in a bank account. Savings that may not be required in the immediate future for products, services, taxes, good works, etc., are available to be treated by the owner as a source of a potential investment. An investment can be thought of as financial resources set aside to be spent in the future. Yet, the range of investments, objectives, and related services, can be mind-boggling for many. An entire industry has arisen that seeks to benefit from this complexity and potential for confusion. As you might guess, I have found it to be useful to begin from a Buddhist perspective when coming to understand this fairly complicated subject matter.

Investing tends to be associated with a specific objective: to have those financial resources that are invested result in more financial resources in the future. We can describe this same objective in terms associated with Right Livelihood: investing can be understood as forgoing the support of value delivery processes in the capacity of a spender today, in the hopes of being able to provide more support of value delivery processes in the future. Though not supporting the reduction of suffering and increase of happiness today as a spender, we can support this value creation today as an investor. Our savings make possible the behaviour of companies and government organizations. Our savings, in whatever form, can be seen as enabling the creation and delivery of value, as well as the creation and delivery of harm.

By enabling these systems with our savings, we, our friends, our family, the local community, or even the global community, can benefit from the value that these systems may provide. As well, these stakeholders can be harmed by processes, and, therefore, are harmed by our support.

Moreover, we ourselves have the potential to receive value for this contribution. The form of value we may receive for our support is in the form of a financial reward, or return on the savings we provide. The idea of an investment includes this sort of potential outcome. As savings result from livelihood, and investments result from savings, I understand investing to be an extension of Right Livelihood behaviour. In other words, we are engaging in Right Livelihood to the extent that our investments reduce suffering, increase happiness, and do not produce harm. As investors, we are stakeholders in the processes being supported, the potential for value creation, and including value in the form of our own financial reward.

From this Buddhist perspective, I also propose that we understand our potential financial reward as a potential means value and not an ends value. Receiving a return on investment does not by itself necessitate that a reduction of suffering or increase in happiness has resulted. Investment returns, indeed all money, if they have value, have a means value. The value is in the possibility that funds could be used for/spent on processes that have ends value: the products and services that actually reduce suffering and increase happiness.

This distinction is critical when it comes to investing mindfully. For, I believe, investors sometimes struggle to balance and weigh the potential ramifications of their investments: harm created or a lack of value created vs (potential) financial reward. They may overlook the fact their investing increases suffering and reduces happiness on balance to all stakeholders, because it produces a financial reward for themselves. This approach is counterproductive, since the only value that financial reward has is to reduce suffering and increase happiness. The investor is failing to recognize that they are not distinct from those that are being harmed, or failing to receive value. By taking a short-sighted approach, our behaviour may result in a net loss of happiness and net increase in suffering for ourselves, regardless of the financial reward.

In this way, investing, and, especially, investing mindfully as an extension of our Right Livelihood behaviour, can be seen as endeavouring to receive value ourselves. Investing mindfully is not about investing just so others can benefit. However good we might feel about ourselves when investing mindfully, there is a real value that we can enjoy far beyond those feelings. From this perspective, I propose that best way to measure the success of any particular investment includes a consideration of both the financial reward or benefit received by the investor and the amount of value generated for all stakeholders. The success of an investment can be measured by the extent to which it enables value delivery processes that result in the reduction of suffering and increase in happiness, on balance, to all.

This idea of investing as being about the benefit to ourselves as well as to others is associated in the financial services industry, as well as in popular culture, with a variety of expressions. These include: ethical investing, socially responsible investing, environmentally responsible investing, impact investing, and more. Regardless of the range of expressions used, an investor who is moved to invest mindfully will typically be engaged in one or more of three basic approaches. These are avoidance approach, positive approach, and activist approach.

With the avoidance approach, the prospective investor is being mindful of the organizations seeking support from investors and identifying something about those organizations that they find repulsive. Perhaps the prospective investor is repulsed by the products and services provided by those organizations. Perhaps it is felt that those products and services do not produce real value to consumers, or actually harm consumers. Additionally, that prospective investor may determine the processes which provide the alleged value also result in harm, suffering or unhappiness for other stakeholders. These undesired outcomes may include harm to the environment, suffering for the employees, and unhappiness for the community. With the avoidance approach, the mindful investor is simply avoiding an investment that is understood to enable or support those outcomes. This approach is also known as screening, as in screening out undesirable processes and the associated organizations. For example, the investor could simply chose to avoid purchasing shares related to a company, or avoid purchasing a bond issued by a government organization.

With the positive approach, the prospective investor is being mindful of the organizations seeking support from investors and identifying something about those organizations that they find attractive. They find something that they want to support. Perhaps the investor feels that the product or service brings considerable value to consumers. Additionally, the prospective investor may feel that the organization's processes are also resulting in value to other stakeholders. Perhaps the organization has systems that bring happiness and success to employees, or improve environmental conditions, or bring value to the community at large. For example, investors could seek out and purchase shares related to a company they want to acknowledge and support, or purchase bonds issued by a level of government they would like to support.

The third approach is known as the activist approach. With this approach, the prospective investor is again being mindful of the organizations seeking support from investors, and again identifying something about their products, services or processes that they find repulsive. However, instead of avoiding or screening out those investments, they are choosing to invest anyway. The activist investor is choosing to make the investment because they want to have the opportunity to encourage a change in the repulsive behaviour. It is believed that they are better positioned to do that if they have a financial stake in that organization. For example, the activist investor may purchase shares of a company and, as such, seek an opportunity to address leadership and solicit change. They might do this by speaking at an annual general meeting, or by sending written communications to the company's leadership or the investor relations department.

A variation of this third approach occurs when the investor is obliged to own a particular investment. This might occur if the investor is an institution and is required by the parameters of their investing activity to hold (for example) a particular stock. It might be the case that they disapprove of specific aspects of the operations of the company associated with that stock, but are unable to screen out that investment. Instead, they may use their ownership of that stock (which represents an ownership in that company) to vote for change when the opportunity arises. They may even encourage other owners to do the same.

How meaningful are these approaches?

When we consider whether or not livelihood behaviour may be morally acceptable, from a Buddhist perspective, we consider whether or not that behaviour is meaningfully contributing to the reduction of suffering or increase in happiness. That is, we consider whether or not true value results. I have argued throughout this book that merely not causing harm by our behaviour is an insufficient form of measurement. We can sit in our basement, not engage the world, and do little harm, but what would be the point of that? As well, when we consider whether or not our behaviour as a spender is morally acceptable, we consider whether or not true value results. So, when we consider whether or not our behaviour as a saver or investor is morally appropriate, we can also consider whether or not true value results. The crux of the matter is whether or not a particular investment or lack of investment, regardless of the approach, would actually advance those objectives deemed laudable by the investor. They could ask:

- Would the investment actually enable and support a value delivery processes?
- Would the investment actually influence an organization to reduce harm or increase happiness?
- Or is the investment activity merely symbolic?

I propose that, by this measurement, sometimes these ethical approaches to investing are indeed influencing, and therefore meaningful. However, in many instances, I believe that they are not meaningful at all. Sometimes such approaches seem to result in little more than having the investor feel good about themselves.

We can understand the relationship between investing and meaningful influence by comparing this activity to spending. Let's suppose that you are contemplating the purchase of a vehicle. When spending mindfully, you would be considering how you might receive value from the purchase of a particular vehicle, what emotional premium you might be paying for (the cost beyond that which is necessary to receive the desired value), and what other stakeholders might receive value or might be harmed by the processes. Let's further suppose that, when shopping and doing your research about which vehicle to purchase, you come to the conclusion that a particular manufacturer is engaging in processes that you deem to be morally inappropriate. So, you refrain from purchasing a vehicle from that manufacturer. In a manner of speaking, you are withholding financial support from those processes. But are you also influencing change? Does the withholding of financial support, by itself, lead to more value creation. It is most unlikely that a manufacturer would ever know that you, personally, refrained from making a purchase. It would not know that you withheld your support, and why, unless you specifically communicated that to them. Moreover, since your particular sentiments may not be representative of the market in general, there is perhaps no good business reason to change even if you did clearly communicate. What might be required to influence change would be many people, not making purchases, and communicating about that to the manufacturer.

Let's suppose, on the other hand, that you identify a vehicle you think will give you the value you are looking for, at price that you believe is appropriate, and with delivery processes that you believe are morally attractive. So, you purchase the vehicle, and, thereby, contribute financially in support of those systems. It is reasonable to believe that such support, especially if it includes similar behaviour of many others, will influence and encourage the manufacturer to some degree. They are receiving your money, and money is a form of reward, a form of influence. However, often vehicles are purchased used. So, let's suppose that a person you don't know purchased a vehicle from a manufacturer several years ago. That person then sold the vehicle to another person you don't know, who used it for a while, before giving it to their child. The child, who you also do not know, used it for a while, and is now hoping to sell it to you. Whether you refrain from purchasing the vehicle or go ahead and purchase the vehicle, how would that meaningfully influence the manufacturer? How would they come to know about what you are doing, or not doing, and why? In fact, I propose it would be much more meaningful to know about the person selling you the car, since that is actually the person that would receive your financial support. It is the behaviour of the seller of the vehicle that you are enabling, and potentially influencing in a much more meaningful way than the manufacturer.

This sort of thinking and behaviour related to the purchase of a vehicle can be applied to the purchase of an investment. The wonderings that arise, like how to think about influence as it relates to new or used purchases, also arise with respect to making an investment. This is because, for the majority of investors, the majority of the investments they are likely to purchase will be used. The distinction between a new investment and a used investment is described in the capital markets as a distinction between a primary market activity and a secondary market activity.

When a business or government is in need of financial resources to help with their processes, they can have an investment created. When these investments (like a stock or a bond) are created and sold to an investor, most of the funds go to the organization that is in need of those resources. This is called a primary market distribution. The proceeds of the sale of investments bring funds to the processes involved in the manufacturing and distributing of the investment as well. Therefore, investment activities are bringing value to manufacturers and distributors of investments. Mindful investing would include being aware of this outcome and support. However, most of the proceeds go to the organization that had the investment created. In a primary market distribution, the funds you provide actually go to the organization that could actually use those funds to advance its value delivery processes. In a meaningful way, your savings could directly support the increase in happiness or reduction of suffering.

However, most investors, most of the time, will not participate in the primary distribution of an investment. They will participate in the secondary market. That is, they will be purchasing an investment that is owned by another investor. The other investor, whether it is a person or an institution, receives those funds. In a meaningful way, those funds are supporting and enabling the behaviour of that selling investor, whether morally acceptable or not. Importantly, with a secondary market investment transaction, the buyer will typically never know who the seller is. If you purchase shares of a Canadian bank, for example, the seller of those shares could be almost anyone, anywhere; it could be a person, a company, or even an institutional investor (like a mutual fund). Your money could go to a person engaged in Right Livelihood, or to a person engaged in the most repulsive forms of behaviour you can imagine.

I am not arguing that there is absolutely no opportunity to exercise some influence when making a secondary market investment. The executives of a large, publicly traded company, whose shares are available to you, do care what you think about that stock. They do want you to want to purchase it. So they do want you to think that, by purchasing it, you will have more financial resources in the future. However, there is no particular reason to believe that they would ever know about your investment purchase, or about the values you have, or about what aspects of that company's value delivery process you like or do not like. Your opportunity to communicate to those executives meaningfully, and therefore have an opportunity to meaningfully influence their behaviour, would be very limited or non-existent.

The purchase of secondary market investments could lead to more meaningful opportunities to influence if those purchases are made in significant volume. Whereas as an individual investor, alone, may not wield influence, as a group, that might change. For example, if an investor purchases units in a mutual fund, and that mutual fund is large enough to purchase many shares in a company, a representative of that mutual fund could communicate to the executives of the target company. Such institutional-sized investment organizations could theoretically influence the target company as the amount of potential investment capital they control might be significant. In such circumstances, however, it might not be clear to you, as a unit holder, what those communications might entail. You might never know which changes are being encouraged, or what values are motivating that encouragement. You might ask:

- Is the mutual fund (or other institutional investor) attempting to influence change?
- If so, what sort of change?
- What values are motivating that attempt at influence?
- Do I have the same values?

- Is that institutional investor investing mindfully, with a view to improving value delivery?
- Or is it merely interested in the value it would receive in the form of a return on investment?

In more recent years, a significant focus of my business efforts have been directed to smaller businesses. In some cases, these businesses have been in relatively early stages of development. In other cases, they were more seasoned organizations, but were in the midst of some change or redevelopment. These businesses have required capital, and, therefore, the attention of investors. My livelihood has included helping many of these fledgling enterprises pursue their own livelihood initiatives. My opportunity to bring value to them has been predicated on their opportunity to bring value to others. So, my pursuit of Right Livelihood has been an endeavour to help others pursue Right Livelihood for themselves. In some cases, I have attempted to bring value by helping them attract prospective investors. This included assisting them with clarifying and confirming their value proposition, or improving their value delivery processes. In many more cases, my work has featured assisting the entrepreneurs with developing and implementing their communications strategies, so that the market would come to know about these value delivery processes. Sometimes, I was compensated for this work as an employee, and sometimes as a consultant. However, the more significant forms of reward would come when I sought to benefit as an investor.

You may not have many opportunities in your working life to have this sort of livelihood opportunity. However, increasingly, stakeholders are enjoying more opportunity to pursue reward from these early stage businesses as investors. The sector of the Canadian financial services industry that facilitates the flow of savings to such businesses has been enjoying a revolution of sorts. This revolution has been aided in part by regulatory changes, and (what I call) the professionalization of the sector that focuses on private investment

## Investing Mindfully

opportunities. These developments have also been aided by technology and emerging business models that enable an average investor to learn about, and invest in, a host of opportunities that they may never have been exposed to in the past. These investments are primary distribution, which means the investment funds provided actually go to the business and meaningfully support and encourage the value delivery. For me, the ability to make such an investment, and to additionally provide guidance and mentorship when I can, has been an expression of my Right Livelihood in both forms of stakeholder.

How might you apply some of these ideas to your own investing activity?

Generally speaking, here is a summary of investing behaviour categorized by least likely to actually influence value delivery (the increase in happiness and decrease in suffering) to most likely:

1. Purchasing (as an activist) an individual, secondary market investment, associated with a large organization (like a corporation or level of government), without an accompanying activist communications strategy;
2. Purchasing (activist) a primary market investment, from a small business, without an accompanying activist communications strategy;
3. Not purchasing (screening) an individual, secondary market investment, associated with a large organization (like a corporation or level of government), without an accompanying communications strategy;
4. Not purchasing (screening) an individual, secondary market investment, associated with a large organization (like a corporation or level of government), with an accompanying communications strategy;
5. Purchasing (positive) an individual, secondary market investment, associated with a large organization (like a corporation or level of government), without an accompanying communications strategy;

6. Purchasing (as an activist) an individual, secondary market investment, associated with a large organization (like a corporation or level of government), with an accompanying communications strategy;
7. Purchasing (positive) an individual, secondary market investment, associated with a large organization (like a corporation or level of government), with an accompanying communications strategy;
8. Purchasing (positive) as part of a group of investors, secondary market investments, associated large organizations (like a corporation or level of government), without an accompanying communications strategy;
9. Purchasing (positive) as part of a group of investors, secondary market investments, associated large organizations (like a corporation or level of government), with an accompanying communications strategy;
10. Not purchasing (screening) as part of a group of investors, secondary market investments, associated large organizations (like a corporation or level of government), without an accompanying communications strategy;
11. Not purchasing (screening) as part of a group of investors, secondary market investments, associated large organizations (like a corporation or level of government), with an accompanying communications strategy;
12. Not purchasing (screening) a primary market investment, from a small business, without an accompanying communications strategy;
13. Purchasing (activist) a primary market investment, from a small business, with an accompanying communications strategy;
14. Purchasing (positive) a primary market investment, from a small business, with an accompanying communications strategy;

15. Purchasing (positive) a primary market investment, from a small business, with an accompanying communications strategy that features active mentorship and guidance.

I appreciate that this overview might be a bit confusing. It might be useful to visualize the relationship between investment, communication, and influence as being about distance. The farther away from the value processes you are, the louder you must be (including communicating with others, for volume), to be heard, and to increase the likelihood of influence. The closer you are to the value delivery processes as an investor the more likely you are to be heard and to influence.

I believe that such mindful investing and communications can bring value to these organizations. Certainly, a direct contribution of capital in the form of an investment is very useful, but even the withholding of capital, with accompanying communication, can be very helpful feedback to a business or level of government. However, does this form of investment also bring additional value to the investor? Specifically, are you more likely to become wealthy from such mindful, Right Livelihood investing? In my opinion, you are.

I have argued that it is very useful to think of wealth creation as being a by-product of providing an unusual amount of value to an unusual amount of people. I have also stressed that this outcome is unusual by definition. Contributing to the rarity of wealth creation, are the limitations we all have with respect to our abilities to give that value, solve the problems, and increase happiness, and our limitation to multiply this value delivery over an increasing number of beneficiaries. In a meaningful way, investing can help solve this problem.

Our savings that are available for investing are the remaining residual from our livelihood activity, after our spending activity. This residual that is invested, in some manner, has the potential to be magnified into additional value delivery processes, giving an increasing amount of value, to an increasing number of people.

When we are investing mindfully as an extension of Right Livelihood, increasing happiness and reducing suffering, we can benefit from the financial reward that results. By focusing on investment activity that meaningfully supports true value delivery, we are more likely to have the opportunity to participate in that reward, and more likely to experience wealth as a result. On the other hand, investing in support of a process that is not resulting in true value delivery, may ultimately be an investment not receiving a financial reward. These are also processes that, for the same reason, may have trouble attracting and retaining other stakeholders, such as employees and suppliers. As stakeholder awareness and sentiment changes, and stakeholders choose to spend mindfully and engage in Right Livelihood with an expectation of receiving true value, those organizations not delivering value may become increasing financially unviable.

Additionally, in my experience, such mindful investing can increase the likelihood of a successful investment outcome by contributing to the reduction of risk. In the pursuit of financial reward, there is a possibility that the goals will not be realized, and the desired success is not achieved. The causes and conditions that may arise that can contribute to the undesired outcomes can be understood as the risks faced in the endeavours. To the extent that the success of our investment activities are dependent upon the success of these endeavours, we are subject to the same risks. There are certainly occasions when those leading the value delivery processes are not as attentive to the risks as they should be. Perhaps they are more focused on the potential revenue and profit of their organization, and the income and bonuses they might receive. Perhaps they are less inclined to consider the factors that might lead to negative outcomes, or are blissfully unaware of unfolding changes. They may fail to adequately factor the possibilities of changing consumer sentiment, changing economic environments, changing regulatory environments, or a myriad additional possible developments. Perhaps, they take shortcuts with processes, or significantly fail to

## Investing Mindfully

consider the value or harm to all stakeholders, on balance, resulting in devastating boycotts or lawsuits. As much as I have enjoyed identifying problems to solve, and developing processes to solve those problems, in more recent years much of my involvement with business owners, entrepreneurs and leadership, has been with respect to identifying and mitigating risk. It has been my experience that when leadership begins to lose sight of the value proposition and the processes for delivering true value to all stakeholders, the risks begin to rise considerably. When leaderships is most mindful of true value, stakeholders, and Right Livelihood, these risks are reduced. Mindful investing, with a consideration of the value delivery, and influencing leadership towards improvement, can result in a reduction of these risks.

Investing mindfully, in my view, can have a benefit to the investor of both being more likely to participate in the reward produced by value delivery, and less likely to experience devastating outcomes from unidentified and unattended-to risks. I believe that a strong case can be made that this form of Right Livelihood is more likely to result in financial success and even wealth for the investor. In the best of scenarios, the investor empowers organizations that can improve the lives of millions of people, in all parts of the world. Unfortunately, there can be a significant challenge for the would-be wealthy and ethical investor. This perspective I have shared might be acceptable and attractive in theory, but many would find it difficult to successfully apply these ideas, and this philosophical approach to wealth creation, in practice. This challenge arises from the support and the resources that we might need to do so. These resources are often sought from the people, the processes, and products of the financial services industry. Our financial success, therefore, may be significantly influenced by the trustworthiness of this industry.

# 9
# Is the Financial Services Industry Trustworthy?

When we truly care about someone or something, we want that person or organization to aspire to be the best version of itself. We will want this, not for our own needs or desires, or for the benefit that we can receive, but for the benefit that this person or organization will enjoy. In Buddhist terms, we will want that someone or something to aspire to eliminate as much suffering, increase as much happiness, and bring as much value to others as it is able. We will recognize that such accomplishments will bring mutual benefit. I care about the financial services industry in this way. I do not believe that most consumers will experience the financial industry in its best version. Moreover, I am not confident that much of this industry has this aspiration, although there are certainly exceptions.

When it comes to the pursuit of financial success, wealth creation, and wealth maintenance, the question of whether or not the financial services industry is trustworthy can be a very important one. I have argued that it is useful to think of financial success as arising first from participating in value delivery processes. Further, I have suggested that, by spending mindfully (focusing on the real value we need, paying as little in tax as legally possible, being very careful with funding charities), we can benefit by having residual savings. These savings can be magnified as investment into (potentially) vast value delivery and wealth creation opportunities.

The participants of the financial services industry will communicate in such a way as to have us be confident that it can bring value to all of these pursuits. Should we, as consumers, have such confidence?

I have attempted to articulate the idea of trustworthiness in a very specific way. Being worthy of trust is understood as being worthy of the confidence in both ability and integrity being sought from the would-be trusting parties by the party desiring trust. This confidence is understood as being in the ability of the party seeking trust to deliver the value as it proposes, and in having the integrity to actually follow through and do so. That the participants of the financial services industry have communicated effectively to establish trust with some of the intended audience is certain. Being trusted (descriptive: what is or is not), however, is far from being trustworthy (normative: what should be or should not be). Determining trustworthiness must begin, therefore, with a consideration of the value propositions. For these are the essence of what is or is not to be trusted. What value does the representative of the financial services industry propose to provide?

When a consumer engages with a product or service provider in any sector of the financial services industry, it would be reasonable to believe that they do so to receive some value. The consumer is looking to have a problem solved, perhaps even to the point of increasing happiness. Some of these problems are fairly easy to identify, even if we do not typically think about them. For example, the financial services industry facilitates payments through debit cards, credit cards, electronic transfers, cheques, etc. This allows us to receive reward for the value we provide as we engage in our livelihood, and it allows us to spend some of this reward to receive value from the livelihood of others. Without such services, we would have a problem: keeping, protecting, and moving hard currency. The proposed value of this part of the financial services industry is to eliminate that problem, for a fee. This value is a means value, rather than an ends value: assisting with the moving of

## Is the Financial Services Industry Trustworthy?

money itself does not reduce suffering or increase happiness. Those potential outcomes result from the spending or investing of those funds. From communications strategy and experience, we develop confidence that such service providers typically have the ability to provide this service. Many of us will also develop confidence that these service providers will typically act with integrity by successfully providing the service when called upon, and even satisfactorily addressing and fixing mistakes along the way. Based upon the value proposition, and the experience I have personally had with this sort of service, I have confidence in their ability and integrity. I have arrived at a state of trust, and believe such service providers are worthy of that trust.

On the other hand, as consumers, we may also be inclined to consider more complicated products and services, such as those related to realizing financial success, and achieving and managing wealth. Representatives of the financial services industry communicate that their processes include bringing these sorts of value to consumers as well. To begin to assess the trustworthiness of the financial services industry in this regard, it is useful to first consider the needs, wants and problems of consumers, and then the relevant related value propositions of financial institutions. When it comes to the pursuit of financial success, and the realization of and maintenance of wealth, what are our needs and wants? Here are a few:

- We want to know what to do, so that we do not suffer from financial hardship, resulting in unrealized human needs, and, therefore, declining happiness and potential suffering;
- We want to know what to do, to achieve more advanced human needs, that result in increased levels of happiness;
- We want to know what to do, and what products to purchase, that result in the ability to have more financial resources in the future, that will result in receiving more value in the future;
- We want to know what to do, and what products to purchase, that result in financial success, as we define it;

- We want to know what to do, and what products to purchase, that contribute to value delivery processes, resulting not in harm, but in the reduction of suffering and increase in happiness, on balance, to all stakeholders;
- We want to know what to do, and what products to purchase, to allow us to participate in an unusual amount of value delivery to an unusual amount of people, resulting in wealth;
- We want to know what to do, and what products to purchase, to allow us to maintain, and perhaps transfer, that wealth.

In the pursuit of the needs and wants, we face problems, such as:
- Limited financial resources (only so much money, priorities of spending and investing is required);
- Limited motivation (we would rather do something else other than to think about and address our financial matters);
- Limited time (too busy with our livelihood and other obligations);
- Limited information and understanding (financial matters can be complicated).

The financial services industry has a long history of developing processes to address these needs, wants and problems. The value propositions tend to be similar among the participants, with the occasional show of more classic entrepreneurial efforts. However, these value propositions may not be clearly stated, and may need to be inferred from communications and behaviour. For example, with respect to addressing our problems, a financial institution and/or its representatives might be understood as proposing:
- We can help you prioritize how to allocate your financial resources, by helping you create a financial plan;
- We can help you keep on track with that plan by prompting you;
- We will take on some of the related tasks (such as research or administration), and may even come to visit you at a time and

## Is the Financial Services Industry Trustworthy?

location convenient for you, to allow you to have more time;
- We will gain the education and knowledge required, and provide you with clear ideas so that you can make informed decisions.

Moreover, with respect to addressing our needs and wants, the financial institutions and representatives craft products and services providing value that may be stated as:
- We can provide products and services (such as insurance) designed to address and mitigate risk, so that you are less likely to experience suffering from financial hardship;
- We can provide services (such as financial planning and investments) that will help you achieve financial success;
- We can provide lending products (mortgage, loans, lines of credit, credit cards) that will allow you to achieve your financial goals;
- We can provide investment advice that will result in more financial resources in the future, net of fees, than would have otherwise been realized;
- We can provide investment products that will result in more financial resources in the future, net of fees, than would have otherwise been realized;
- We can provide investment products and services (such as estate planning) that will result in the maintenance and transfer of that wealth, that, net of fees, will result in more financial resources than would have otherwise been realized.

What's that, you say? You don't typically experience such clearly communicated value propositions from a financial institution or representative?

Therein lies one of the more significant difficulties in assessing their trustworthiness. If the value proposition is not clear, we cannot determine whether or not they have the ability or the integrity to deliver. Indeed, if we are not sure what the proposed value is, we will not have a meaningful way to measure the success of their proposed value delivery processes. I believe that many communications strategies in the financial services industry do not feature a clear value position, but are designed to have us arrive at states of confidence – states of trust – by other means.

Branding, as an element of communications strategy, is very important to financial institutions. These brands result in feelings of confidence and trust, even when there is not specific evidence to support them. The intention is that we arrive at feelings regarding their ability and integrity, even when the message does not provide specific information, to produce a state of knowledge that the value proposition (whatever it may be) will actually be delivered. Sometimes an institution or representative will propose that its products or services will lead to comfort, confidence, feelings of security, and the like. It may be suggested, for example, that those who use financial services of a particular institution report feeling more confident in their retirement plan.

As I have stated, I propose that feelings are not, in and of themselves, a value. Feelings of confidence and comfort may result from there being good reason to have those feelings, or they may result from a false sense of security, or an inability to recognize and assess one's financial circumstances. What may be of real value to a consumer is an actual set of financial circumstances that can reasonably be expected to produce the desired retirement, not merely a feeling that everything will unfold as hoped. True value is about the actual realization of increased happiness and reduced suffering, not a feeling that one need not worry, and that everything will be alright.

From this perspective, the assessment of the trustworthiness of the financial services industry must begin with having consumers being able to clearly identify and communicate their financial needs and wants, and to understand and share the problems they face in these pursuits. As described, success can be understood as the accomplishment of goals. Financial success can be understood

## Is the Financial Services Industry Trustworthy?

as the accomplishment of our financial goals. If we want to be financially successful, we must be able to clearly identify these goals, so that we can measure when they have been realized. If we believe it is worthwhile to consider whether or not a financial institution or representative can bring value in these endeavours, we would benefit from being able to communicate these goals clearly as well. It is in response to such goals, and our own understanding of financial success, that a value proposition can be presented. We must insist that the proposed value is clearly stated – first, to determine whether it is the value we are looking for (in light of our goals), and second, to be able to determine, based on evidence, whether or not the offering party has the ability and the integrity to deliver: that is, to determine whether or not the offering party should be deemed trustworthy.

There are myriad possible financial goals, and, potentially, as many expressions of financial success as there are people hoping to achieve it. Even coming to a decision as to what our goals are, or even what they should be, can be difficult for some. Such folks may even look to the representatives of the financial services industry for guidance about this as well.

Therein lies a second significant difficulty in assessing the trustworthiness of the financial services industry. A great number of the representatives are not trained, motivated, or compensated to help us decide what is important to us, or to help us clarify our values, our priorities, or the financial goals that may arise from these. They are, however, trained and compensated to sell us something. Many become very skilled at encouraging us to set specific goals, or to think of financial success in particular ways. This skill helps them to have consumers understand that the financial products and services being sold are the solution to the problem that they would like us to identify. For example, those selling risk management or risk mitigation products, like insurance, may want us to identify remote, unlikely occurrences, like premature death, as a problem requiring attention, and as a priority. Those that are compensated to provide credit (credit cards, loans, mortgages, etc.) may want us have financial goals that feature the purchase of something that we do not have sufficient financial resources to acquire. They may want us to define financial success as owning material possessions (like cars and consumer goods) that we cannot entirely pay for currently. It is critical that we, as consumers and goal-setters, attend mindfully and diligently to the determination of our own wants, needs and priorities.

This determination of the value we might actually seek from a financial institution or representative is not only for our own benefit. By clarifying and communicating to such parties, we are helping to enable them to deliver the true value we seek. It helps them to respond with a proposal of value in the form of products and services that might actually reduce our suffering and increase our happiness as we define them. We help to enable those representatives to engage in Right Livelihood.

Even without articulating very specific goals, priorities, wants, needs, and problems of individual consumers, there are general statements of value that seem to have application with the consumer market. I will consider some of these general statements as part of this assessment of trustworthiness, so that considerations of ability and integrity can be included. Generally speaking, when it comes to wealth creation and management, we tend to be seeking a similar value:

We seek financial products and services that will result in more future financial resources than we would have achieved without those products and services, net of the cost of those products and services.

To be fair, I believe consumers are often seeking more than a marginal increase in future financial resources, but are actually seeking relative financial success, as they define it. Many are seeking to have improving circumstances, achieving better than average results, and even realizing wealth. It might even be reasoned that it is not advantageous to pay for products and services which bring

## Is the Financial Services Industry Trustworthy?

no additional financial benefit beyond achieving a state of average financial success.

In response to this sort of value being sought, financial institutions may be seen as offering value (even if it is not clearly stated) featuring services that include ideas, information, and planning services, and value in the form of investment products and services. A determination of whether or not the financial services industry should be considered trustworthy must include a consideration of whether or not there is evidence to support the confidence that the institutions and representatives actually have the ability to deliver this value. What are their actual abilities?

My experience of financial services organizations is that they tend to be populated with average people. (Again, to be clear, I welcome average abilities and performance, for they make possible the measurement of the exceptional.) The majority of these persons tend not to be empowered with unusual skills, ability, or education that would enable them to provide unusual value to consumers. Indeed, many have very modest levels of experience. They most certainly tend not to be successful business persons, or entrepreneurs, poised to achieve unusual financial success themselves. It is hard for me to imagine that many possess the ability to empower others with the information and ideas they might need to achieve more ambitious degrees of financial success and wealth. I imagine that, if they had such ability, they would be seeking to benefit from that themselves. In fact, as a rule of thumb, the greater their ability, the less likely you are to meet them, and receive their value. Those of greater ability tend to be promoted away from client-facing roles, or leave the institution you are a client of, for better opportunity elsewhere.

Even in roles that are presented as specializations to consumers (such as those related to specific areas of expertise or investment products and services), very often the educational requirement is very minimal. Many consumers engage with financial representatives whose role is granted based upon passing a single course, completed in a few days or weeks. Consumers may optimistically arrive a state of confidence that the representative has the ability to deliver value in the form of financial success and wealth creation based upon that single course.

Certainly some financial representatives, and especially investment advisors, achieve much more significant education and ability. There are some who commit many years in completing very difficult courses that lead to advanced designations. Sometimes these designations require specific forms of work experience. Additionally, those with greater abilities and more experience may seek to be vetted and assessed by provincial regulatory bodies in pursuit of permission to engage in more advanced forms of livelihood. This approval and permission is represented by being granted a category of registration. Sometimes these registration categories are associated with specific titles (like Chief Compliance Officer), which may provide additional evidence in support of arriving at a state of ability trust. Unfortunately, consumers would be wise not to automatically infer too much ability, and have too much trust, based upon the title and letters after the name on a business card, or on social media. Presenting an ever-lengthening series of letters after a name as evidence of ability is prevalent. Such letters should not constitute sufficient evidence without a clear understanding of what those letters represent. (I have even heard such alphabet soup cleverly described as looking like "the sound a person might make when they are dying.") Similarly, one should not conclude from the presence of an impressive title that a person is of more than average ability.

Moreover, historically, one of the great ironies of pursuing value from a financial representative of unusual ability is that the farther you are from financial success and wealth, and, therefore, the more you might benefit from their value, the less likely you are to actually have the opportunity to receive that value from them. In the more extreme cases, it has been my experience that those with the greatest ability, and most able to provide the value of financial success and wealth, are least in need of clients and least in need of that form of livelihood. They have used those skills and abilities to achieve their own wealth.

There will be times when you, as a consumer, are presented with a value proposition that is based on the product being sold, rather than the seller of that product. The communication may feature the idea that, though the seller may be of modest ability, the creators and managers of the products are exceptional, and, therefore, the product can deliver exceptional value. When it comes to investment products, such a proposal should be met with increasing skepticism. There is a commonly proposed value to the market, when it comes to investments: that the product, based upon the skills of its creators and managers, can deliver more value (i.e., more financial resources in the future), net of the fees being charged, than the consumer could achieve by not purchasing the product.

When it comes to publicly traded, secondary market investments (described as used investments, earlier), the specific value proposition of the related managers and investment advisors tends to focus on two features. First, they propose that they have the ability to identify and select specific investments producing more financial value than other managers, and more financial value than the consumer would have realized making their own choices. Second, they propose that the manager can continue to manage, rebalance and look for opportunities in a manner bringing more value to the consumer than that provided by other managers, or by the consumer attempting to do this on their own. Additionally, in each case, the value proposition includes the idea that the value they can provide to the consumer is net of fees. That is, they will charge the client for the services, but the client will still experience more future financial resources regardless. There are numerous concerns I have with the proposed ability of investment product manufactures and advisors to deliver this proposed value. I will limit the description of these concerns to those I deem most dire.

There is a view held to some degree or another by a great number of very bright and objective observers of investment markets.

The proposal is that, due to the timely and global availability of information and analysis, those that manage investments have access to the same information. The quality, quantity and timelessness of this information, and the ability to respond to this information (enabled by shared technology), is resulting in increasing market efficiency. From this perspective, it is believed that the prices of public investments result from very broad and considered consensus. Or, simply, stated, the securities are priced correctly, or very, very close to correctly. The implication is that the expected future value, and therefore, the likely return to the investor is already factored into that price.

The idea that an analyst is going to find some publicly disclosed information, leading to some insight that has not already been seen, acted upon, and reflected in the public valuation of that investment, is quaint and unrealistic. What value is the manager of those funds bringing to the investor that is not already available to everyone? Indeed, receiving and acting upon information that is not disclosed and available to everyone may be considered a crime: insider trading. In fact, those who regulate and police the securities markets will typical report that their mandate features the creation of fair and efficient markets. The more efficient the markets, the less value investment managers are thought to be able to deliver.

This perspective, in my opinion, should have consumers calling into question the value proposition (as it has historically been presented) of entire swaths of the financial services industry. It challenges the notion that an investment manager (any manager) of publicly traded securities can consistently select specific investments that result in better performance than other managers, and even better than what most investors can do on their own. Bearing in mind, even if an investment manager can provide better results even some of the time, those results have to be much better, as they have to take into account the costs to the investor. For example, let's suppose that the stock market in general, or a basket of stocks more or less representing the stock market, had been producing a

## Is the Financial Services Industry Trustworthy?

gain to investors (before tax) of 5% per year. Now, let's suppose that a mutual fund manager proposes to purchase specific stocks and charge an investor a fee of 2.5% per year. That means, the mutual fund would have to realize returns of over 7.5%, so that the investor could experience a return better than if they had just purchased the securities without such help. The investment manager would have to produce returns more than 50% better than the market in general. It is this ability that is being challenged, and so, this form of trustworthiness being called into question. Interestingly, proponents of this view of efficient markets do propose that there may be some exceptions – specifically when the investment manager is able to include alternative products and strategies. Such alternatives may include non-public (private, primary market) investments and hedging strategies, such as options.

This view of public investments, and costs related to the management of public investments, helps to explain one of the more significant trends in recent years: the rising popularity of exchange traded funds (ETF's). Such products provide exposure to public markets (with some similarities to traditional mutual funds) but for a much lower cost. The premise of the value position of such products seems to include: if you can't consistently achieve better performance in publicly traded securities net of fees, just try lowering the fee. Or, put another way, if the value proposition of the fund manager (a service at a specific price) does not provide the actual value sought by the consumer, the value proposition needs to change.

Interestingly, the response from many in the financial services industry to this phenomena, however, has not been to lower the price appropriately to be in line with the value (or lack of value) actually received by the consumer. The response has been to keep the same fee (or lower it slightly), but suggest that the value from that fee is actually different than what we have understood it to be. The historic value proposition understood by investors in mutual funds, for example, would have been described as:

professional management and securities selection, resulting in a diversified basket of securities that will produce better results than purchasing them oneself. However, it seems to me, as the viability of this value position has been increasingly challenged, and the ability and trustworthiness of the related financial representatives on this matter increasingly called into question, the proposed value is being altered. It is increasingly being suggested that, the cost of owing such funds, which is paid for by the consumer through periodic management expenses, is actually to cover the cost of financial planning advice. Consumers are being told that the value proposition includes both investment management services and financial planning, bundled together. This begs the original question: do the advisors actually have the ability to provide you with ideas and information that will enable you to achieve financial success as you envision it? Though many are now paying for such a proposed value, are they actually receiving it?

Even if the financial representative had the ability to provide such value, the systems in which they conduct their livelihood might make it extremely difficult, or nearly impossible, to provide the value that you might be expecting. Historically, it seems to me that a great number of investment salespersons allowed consumers to believe that part of their role was to help those consumers purchase investments at an attractive price (low, for example) and sell at a better price (high) to realize a profit. Further, consumers might come to believe during the relationship that perhaps the investment representative will prompt them when to make changes to their investment portfolio to capitalize on market opportunities. If you believe, as I anticipate many do, that this is the sort of value or service you might reasonably expect, you may be surprised. To clarify, I will relate an experience that I had.

During 2007 and 2008, I had been researching, writing and speaking about investment markets and demography. The ideas I was sharing were not particularly sophisticated or insightful. I wrote a paper entitled *Move It or Lose It*, and was giving lectures

## Is the Financial Services Industry Trustworthy?

with the same title. Part of the message was that there were concerns the stock market might experience a decline, and that it might be disturbing to investors. Moreover, I was proposing that, given the age of baby boomers and their proximity to retirement, a market decline might be more disturbing than previous declines. The presentation also discussed how private investments might provide some protection against a decline. The last time I gave the speech was in Las Vegas. The following day the internationally known investment bank, Lehman Brothers, announced its bankruptcy. The stock market declined very significantly. The presentations that I had been doing were primarily to audiences of investment advisors. They were attending classes, and, theoretically, gathering information and opinions to improve themselves professionally and assist their clients. You might think that such professionalism should be expected, and that the investment advisors were pleased to have heard these ideas before the market decline. You might even expect that their clients were very glad that their advisors were provided with such ideas. I suggest, you would be more wrong than right.

On one very memorable occasion, I was giving this lecture, and I could see from the podium the outline of a figure moving around at the back of the room. I would quickly come to realize that this person was very agitated by my message. He presented himself aggressively to me after the presentation. He was big, angry, and it is not an overstatement to say that I felt threatened. He suggested that I was being irresponsible with my message, and even suggested that I was fear-mongering. I anticipate that many advisors felt similarly agitated by my message, even if they did not express it as he did. I am very sympathetic, actually. What was he supposed to do with that message? Even if he thought that some of my ideas had merit, what could he do about it?

The working environment for a great number of investment advisors makes responding to information and change, in a way that provides value that many investors are looking for, extremely difficult. First, many advisors will direct investors to investment funds that purchase specific assets in a specific geographic location: like a fund that might purchase stock that is publicly traded in a particular country, like the USA or Canada. The fund managers are typically limited to the purchase of these stocks regardless of market conditions. That is, they must keep buying, even if the prices are considered high, and even if there are better opportunities with other investments, in other sectors, from other parts of the world and economic circumstances. The fund managers might actually wish they could buy other investments, or even sell the ones they have, at a profit, hold a cash position, and wait for prices to become better. They might even want to position themselves to take advantage of serious market corrections by buying low and selling high. Alas, they cannot. They are stuck with the limited focus of the fund. So, when an investment advisor sells such a fund to a consumer, the advisor is putting the investment decisions into the hands of the manager. What that advisor might learn at a conference, or think about my perspective on market conditions and opportunities, will have no bearing on what the fund manager can or will do with the fund.

Rather than changing the investments within the investment fund, which the investment advisor cannot do, perhaps that advisor could have the client move from one investment fund to a different fund. Perhaps by doing so, the client would effectively be selling one set of securities to buy another set, to take advantage of changing market conditions. Unfortunately, that advisor would face a variety of issues and obstacles. For example, such investment advisors are typically required to communicate to each client directly. They would have to present their recommendations for change, and have the clients agree to the changes (typically with a signature). They are not able to simply move the client's money around into different investments as they like. So, they have to get to every client. They may have hundreds of clients, and market conditions can change quickly. So, whom do they contact first? Their parents? Their largest clients? The clients that can bring the most new revenue to them? What makes you think it would be you? What makes you think they would ever get to you? Or if they did, the market may have already changed, and the investments may have already declined in value. In these scenarios, the investment industry can be expected, as a whole, to be of more benefit to those who already have more money and influence.

However, let's imagine that such an advisor, having come to sense that the market was about to change, and had enough time, and few enough clients, to actually get to all of them, make the recommendations and implement the changes. Unfortunately, there are systemic disincentives discouraging this behaviour. For example, the advisor must adhere to strict compliance and regulatory protocol. Being seen as not having done so is a significant risk to the advisor, and quite possibly to the staff responsible for that advisor's supervision. Additionally, there is typically no income opportunity or reward to offset the risk. Many advisors would not be compensated for making these changes. Moreover, the time it takes to get to all the clients and process all the changes is an opportunity cost; the advisor is not working to attract clients and generating revenue. It gets worse.

Historically, investment advisors are compensated much more for some investment funds than for others. For example, selling a fund of stock from those large publicly traded companies produced much more revenue to the sales person than selling of a fund of very conservative investments, like money market instruments. These conservative investments are the kind of investments an investor might own if they thought the stock market was going to decline. For example, if I had a portfolio of investments that had increased in value as the stock market went up, and I wanted to preserve that return, and I thought the market was going to decline (as I did in 2008), I could sell those investments and then purchase money market instruments in a fund. If the stock market declined, I could then sell the money market fund and buy back into the stock fund at the new, lower, prices. Effectively, I would have bought low, sold high, and bought low again. Isn't that how it's supposed to work? Well, typical investment advisors – the kinds that a typical retail investors would experience – are compensated much, much higher when their clients owns those stock funds, rather than money market funds. The investment advisor is compensated in the form of a trailer, or trailing commission. For many investment advisors, the bulk of their monthly income comes from these trailers. If they have their clients sell those stock funds to buy money market funds, the trailers can be lowered very dramatically. As such, the decision to have a client sell those stock funds high, and then wait for a while, to see if the stock market declines, before buying back in, would actually cost that investment advisor. By the way, the compensation to the manager of that investment advisor may also be tied to the amount of money invested in those stock funds. A decision to advise an entire client base to make such changes is a decision to incur compliance-related risk, opportunity cost (time spent), actual cost (overhead, and potential loss of revenue), and possibly even strained relationships with management. What if that advisor ends up being wrong about market activity?

Even if an investment advisor has the intellectual ability to deliver the value position that many consumers might expect to receive, the actual structure of the business in which many investment advisors find themselves all but reasonably precludes that likelihood. Rather than attempt to deliver this sort of proactive value to consumers, investment advisors, instead, become adept at managing their client's expectation of value retroactively. For example, rather than prompt a rebalancing of investments prior to a market decline, they may tell the client, after the decline, not to change. They are taught to say things like:

- Do not sell now! You will just ensure your loss!
- The market will come back. It always does. Be patient!
- These aren't your numbers! You're not retiring for a long time.
- I told you that the market goes up and down. You said you were okay with that.

## Is the Financial Services Industry Trustworthy?

Another tactic an investment advisor might use to retroactively manage a client's assessment of value occurs when a client tries to prompt a comparison between the performance of their investments and the performance of other investments. This is most likely to occur when the client identifies other (similar) investments as having better returns. An advisor may be taught to say:

"Yes, your investment fund provided you with a 4% rate of return, while that other similar investment would have provided you with a 7% rate of return. That other fund must have taken on considerably more risk. Do you really want to take on more risk?"

Investment representatives and consumers are encouraged to accept the relationship between risk and reward as a constant truism. They are encouraged to think that higher returns to the consumer could have only resulted from higher risks. Yet, higher returns to consumers could have also resulted from factors such as lower costs, more skilled fund management, and the flexibility of the fund management to consider a variety of securities and strategies. This flexibility might include being able to purchase the aforementioned alternatives, such as private securities and options.

This brings us to a third significant difficulty in assessing the abilities of a financial institution or financial representative: the limitations on what kinds or products and services they can sell.

The financial services industry tends to silo individuals into particular sectors, with specific licenses and registration categories. These licenses and registrations dictate the sorts of products they are permitted to present, and the manner in which they can be presented. Licences and registrations are typically sponsored by a financial services organization that takes responsibility for the representative, and provides them with a range of products and services. These products and services are often manufactured by that financial services organization, or are featured with a limited set of products manufactured by other organizations. As such, typical financial representatives, regardless of how they may attempt to present themselves to consumers, are limited in the solutions they can provide. For example, though my *Move It or Lose It* presentations included a discussion of the relative merits of private securities, the vast majority of the investment representatives who might have heard my message would have been precluded from making such recommendations to their clients. This limitation is dictated by their registrations, licenses, and the rules and financial institutions and regulatory bodies that control their livelihood. The implication is that, regardless of their intellectual ability, the livelihood situation and systems of financial representatives dictate the forms of value they are actually able to provide. Almost every single participant in the financial services industry faces this sort of limitation.

I do not believe, by these measurements, that consumers should generally have confidence in the ability of a typical investment advisor. I believe that, generally, the financial services industry is not trustworthy in this regard. What about trustworthiness with respect to integrity?

Integrity trust is the form of confidence that a consumer might have that a value which can be provided will actually be provided. The trustworthiness of a financial institution or a financial representative includes an assessment of whether or not that institution or person will fulfill the promise of their value proposition and deliver that value as we have come to expect they will. This assessment considers real action and behaviour. As I have defined it, integrity can be understood as an alignment of that behaviour with the values of the acting party, as we have come to understand those values.

Therein lies a fourth significant problem in determining trustworthiness of the financial services industry: the values of the institution or representative are not clearly communicated. Instead, consumers are often left to assume values, the way we might assume those driving their car next to ours down the highway have values similar enough to our own. For example, we may assume the representatives of financial institutions with whom we engage have values that we might expect them to have when conducting their livelihood with us: honesty, privacy, informed decision making, helping us address our needs and solve our problems.

I imagine that many enter the financial services industry with these sorts of values, and perhaps even with some naiveté. They might believe that their livelihood will feature completing some form of administrative task, or providing some guidance and instruction, or creating a financial plan, or providing investment advice. A great number will come to realize that their compensation, recognition, and advancement is not based on completing administration, or providing instruction, planning, or advice. The incentive, including remaining employed, is dependent upon the consumer purchasing a product or service. The vast majority of financial planners I have met over decades as a manager and trainer, for example, do not charge a fee to a client for providing advice or creating a financial plan. They are paid when the client purchases a product or service. The systems that attract, recruit, recognize and reward financial representatives are designed to support the sale of these products and services.

Those that hire, train, and manage financial representatives also have recognition and reward tied to the sale of products and services. They are incentivized to oversee systems that emphasize the delivery of the outcomes as dictated by the financial goals of the organization. I have never seen a system wherein the consumer's happiness is measured. It would be highly unusual that the compensation of those engaging in livelihood in such systems would be based entirely on the measurement of the end value received by the consumer. In short, much of what seems to go on in the financial services industry is not in support of positive relationships. The financial success of many financial representatives is not actually based upon the success of their clients.

The results of such causes and conditions have disturbed me regularly throughout my career. There is, I believe, a sufficient degree of omission or intellectual dishonesty – even deceit – that should concern consumers. To the extent that reward and recognition systems encourage sales first, and the maximization of consumer value second, I caution all consumers to not assume that the values of the financial institutions and representatives are as they hope they will be.

One might be forgiven for assuming that these incentives and encouragements of behavior are meaningfully muted or mitigated by other forces. Surely there are other rules or laws that sufficiently protect consumers, you might think. Internationally, thought-leaders who influence and direct the regulatory environments, and consider the business models, compensation schemes, and participant responsibilities, continue to discuss the merits of systemic change. While there are the occasional bursts of discussion and sabre-rattling around the need to protect consumers, the kind of political will that may be required to produce significant change seems to be elusive. As such, in my opinion, the expression "buyer beware" remains a useful warning, especially when it comes to the sectors of the financial services industry that provides investments.

In the private market (or exempt market) sectors, for example, the obligations of the company in which you might invest are largely dictated by the disclosing document it provides. Such a document, often called an Offering Memorandum, sets the terms of the relationship, and can provide protection to the company (the issuer) in the event that the business does not unfold as you were lead to believe it may. Additionally, consumers are often required to sign a document acknowledging that the risks of the investment are significant, and may even include catastrophic losses. Regardless of such documents, many have purchased such primary market investments, and have gone on to experience those significant losses. I have personally come to a mistaken state of confidence in such companies, and have come to realize some to be completely unworthy of the trust I bestowed.

The financial institutions and the representatives paid to facilitate the purchase of these private investments, as well as of

## Is the Financial Services Industry Trustworthy?

most public investments, are held to a relatively low legal standard. The standard set is known as a suitability standard. That is, if they encourage an investor to buy an investment that is suitable, they have acted appropriately. To a typical consumer, that standard might seem fine. However, there are other standards that many believe provide greater benefit, and will result in more value, to the consumer. A best interest standard would require that the financial representatives provide the best products and services, or, perhaps, described as the most suitable products and services. The highest standard is considered to be a fiduciary duty: an obligation to put the needs of the consumer ahead of the needs of the representative and the institution. In my mind, this standard may be considered to be a defining characteristic of what it means to be a true professional.

Let's consider some of these ideas by drawing a comparison to another kind of business. Imagine that you have decided that it is your goal to lose weight and to get into shape. You might pursue those objectives by engaging a personal trainer. The personal trainer may provide an assessment of your physical condition, discuss any health issues you may have, discuss nutrition and lifestyle choices you are making. The trainer then recommends various approaches that might include walking, yoga, cycling, weight training, etc., and point you in the direction of various providers. For these services, the trainer charges an hourly rate, and, at any point, if you feel you are not getting value, you can easily terminate the relationship. The trainer helps you measure the progress against the goals, and engages with you regularly, in the hopes that you will remain a client. Their business model emphasizes forming a positive relationship. On the other hand, let's imagine that you have the same goals (to lose weight and get into shape) and, with those goals in mind, you walk into a bike shop. We might expect that the bike salesperson feels no obligation to assess your physical condition, or discuss nutrition. We might expect the bike salesperson to suggest that a bike is a suitable product given your goals, and we might expect that the salesperson's compensation, advancement and continued employability will be tied to the sale of bikes. Perhaps the bike salesperson might help us chose among the limited makes and models available in that store, and may even enjoy further reward and recognition for selling specific brands over others. We would imagine it to be unlikely that the bike salesperson would recommend that we go to a competitor's bike store. We might even imagine that some of the bikes can only be serviced by the store proving the bike, and, so, the purchaser must return to continue to pay for on-going support. Perhaps you felt dissatisfied with this business model as a consumer, and petitioned for improvement. You might not be surprised to see bike manufacturers and distributors rallying together to defend their industry and business models. I doubt that any of us would be surprised to walk into a bike store and have this experience. Yet, it seems that many are still surprised to learn that financial representatives, who are subject to only a suitability standard, often have more in common with the bike salesperson than the personal trainer.

To be fair, there are many in the financial services industry who hold themselves to a higher standard than that of bike salesperson. Such persons may be moved by personal values, or adhere to strict codes of conduct, or adopt codes of ethics with sincerity. Unfortunately, as I have emphasized, many who have such standards, and will act with integrity, are not skilled at communicating that fact. While they may be trustworthy, as it relates to integrity, they may not be clearly providing evidence in support of that form of confidence. On the other hand, it is worrisome that consumers may find that those least worthy of this form of trust, are actually better at communicating.

Consumers of financial products and services, and clients of financial representatives, are justified in being very cautious about the trustworthiness of those with whom they engage. We all are moved by the communications we receive to arrive at various degrees of confidence in their abilities and integrity. In some instances,

## Is the Financial Services Industry Trustworthy?

we may receive the value that we anticipate, and in other instances, we will not. However, we can participate in these engagements to significantly increase the likelihood of receiving value we need, to accomplish our financial goals, and achieve success as we define it. Here are some suggestions:

- Determine clear financial goals, and be prepared to clearly communicate what financial success means to you;
- Be prepared to communicate what problems you believe you face in pursuing this success;
- Be wary of communications that emphasize mere branding and feeling;
- Rather, insist that you receive from a financial institution or representative a clear value proposition, including a clear understanding of cost;
- Insist that you receive sufficient and clear evidence that the institution or representative has the ability to deliver that value as proposed;
- Insist that you receive sufficient and clear evidence that the institution or representative has the integrity to deliver that value as proposed;
- Come to understand how the value delivery systesms of the institution or representative serve to reduce harm, and increase happiness, on balance, to all stakeholders.

As we, as consumers, understand how to engage with financial institutions and their representatives more effectively, and insist that they abandon their often hyperbolic communications strategies for discussions of true needs and the desired value, we can influence change. Such encouragements will not be merely for our own benefit, but will benefit those institutions and representatives. They can be guided towards the pursuit of Right Livelihood – a focus on actually reducing suffering and increasing happiness. We can help guide the industry towards being the best, most trustworthy version of itself. Though often considered to be conservative, slow-moving and staid, this industry has aspects to it that are evolving quickly. As technology is disrupting and threatening value propositions, it is also enabling new business models, and new forms of consumer interaction. Some of these changes are empowering consumers, and enabling the pursuit of financial success and wealth creation, in new ways. I will consider the relationships between change and opportunity next.

# 10
# Impermanence and Opportunity

The premise for Buddhist philosophy stems from a simple observation: that people often experience unhappiness to varying degrees, and even to the point of suffering. The wisdom of the philosophy is that the causes of the unhappiness include wants and desires. The compassion of the philosophy is that we can and should assist ourselves and others with the cessation of suffering, and increase in happiness. Throughout this text, I have presented examples of needs, wants, goals, and aspirations that are typical of most people. Yet one of the more universal, more pervasive causes of unhappiness has yet to be fully addressed. This is the unhappiness and anxiety that can arise from change.

Impermanence is a common theme in Buddhist teachings. That all things, people, circumstances, causes, and conditions will change is another, apparently simple observation. Yet, as with the others, it is an observation that has profound implications for how we might want to think about and respond to our experiences of living. Our responses to the phenomenon of change can be useful and advance our pursuits of happiness, or they can hinder those pursuits. Strictly speaking, it is not change that causes the unhappiness, it is the desire that things not change. It is the want to have those things, people and circumstances remain the same. We can refer to the sort of desire that might lead to unhappiness in the inevitability of change as attachment.

For some, attachment can be thought of as taking our

appreciation of the current states of affairs too far. While it is important to acknowledge and appreciate those aspects of life that are reducing our suffering, and increasing our happiness, it must be recognized that these aspects will change. We should be grateful for that which is bringing us value, and be grateful for when we can bring value to others, but recognize that these circumstances or abilities will change. Indeed, I am more appreciative of that which brings value by being aware of its impermanence. It reminds me to be mindful of those people and things which are bringing me happiness, and to not take this happiness for granted.

For others, there is attachment even when value is not being received. Some will be attached to painful memories of the past, or to people who bring unhappiness and suffering. Some are attached to a vision of a future state of affairs that may or may not materialize, but which precludes finding happiness in the present. Some become attached to forms of livelihood, colleagues, or organizations, and cannot bring themselves to leave these. Some become attached to possessions such as cars and houses that have long out-lived the ability to bring the appropriate degree of value to their lives. I imagine that, for some, the attachment results in part from how we define ourselves, or how we believe others identify us. It might be expected that my father, for example, a career policeman, may have experienced some forms of unhappiness when he retired. He may have so strongly defined himself by his livelihood that it manifested into attachment and led to some suffering when the inevitable impermanence presented itself. It might be reasoned that such defining and attachment lends credence to the Buddhist notion that there is not a self that is meaningfully distinct from everything else. In that vein, we might conclude that, if there is no self that we identify as that which defines us, then we would naturally seek to define ourselves by the company we keep, the place we live, the livelihood we pursue, and the stuff we buy. A loss of the relationships, livelihood and stuff may be felt traumatically as a loss of self. Yet, like others, my father ultimately went on to

## Impermanence and Opportunity

new experiences. Severing attachments, and being able to let go of things, people and circumstances, creates the potential for these new experiences, including receiving value and gratitude.

However, impermanence should be thought as much more than a reminder to be grateful. It is not merely a truism that we must come to deal with and accept. In fact, change can be thought of as a necessary condition to allow the possibility of providing new forms of value to others. That is, the ability for us to engage in Right Livelihood exists because of change. The ability to be rewarded for solving problems exists because new problems emerge. Were it not for change, we would not have new opportunities to provide unusual value to unusual numbers of people, and achieve that unusual form of financial success: wealth.

For entrepreneurs, impermanence is a critical cause of opportunity. People and organizations have been identifying and addressing problems for as long as there have been people and organizations. One might conclude that all of the more meaningful problems have already been addressed. Certainly, many have, and very effectively. Yet, solutions to problems can result in new problems. The ability to take resources from the earth and apply these to satisfying human needs has done much to increase happiness and reduce suffering. Yet, as the solutions have been implemented, new problems arise, such as waste and environmental concerns. Such changes lead to new opportunities for entrepreneurs to bring value and to engage in Right Livelihood.

The value delivery processes change as well. How we go about solving these problems and providing value is impermanent. Human history is punctuated with instances of extraordinary innovation: from the invention of the printing press, through mechanical and systems developments associated with the industrial revolution, and especially the more recent advancements and disruptions associated with contemporary digital technology. How we do what we do is subject to constant change. The implication is that our ability to participate in these processes, and contribute to the value propositions, is also subject to change. This challenges us to learn, adjust, adapt, and improve, to remain a relevant contributor to these processes. Those who cannot or will not do so become those providing declining degrees of value to declining number of people. Conversely, this also creates the opportunity for others to step in, and provide increasing degrees of value, to increasing numbers, and attain the commensurate financial reward.

Products are impermanent. They lose their appeal, or become worn and tarnished, or simply break – like the crystal bowl I dropped during the nativity play. They become considered as obsolete, or outdated, or out of fashion. They are not permanent solutions to problems, and so they are replaced, thereby allowing for value delivery processes to continue. Impermanence allows innovators and entrepreneurs to communicate new proposals of value (their better mousetraps) to a ready audience of consumers. While some needs and wants, theoretically, need addressing only on occasion (a house, a car, a wedding, a university degree), others are considered to be appetites. These are the needs that are only satisfied temporarily, like hunger and thirst, or a desire for entertainment. This form of change presents ongoing opportunities for organizations to communicate their differentiated value propositions, and have us come to know, think, feel, and do in new ways, which leads to new expressions of consumption.

As these processes change, the impact on stakeholders may also change. From changing ways of providing means value and ends value, new forms of harm may emerge. Managers and leaders are tasked and challenged by the changes to consider how these may result in increasing happiness on balance to all. For this reason, it is not useful to think of balance as merely as a noun, or a state of affairs that one can attain. Balance is best thought of as a verb, and a form of action. We do not attain a state of balance, but we are constantly balancing. Due to the inevitability of impermanence and the constancy of change, we are forever adjusting and improving. As such, we continue to have new problems to solve, and new

## Impermanence and Opportunity

ways to pursue Right Livelihood.

More than simply being a responder to change, we can be its instigator, or perhaps even its architect. The phenomenon of change should be an encouragement, as it presents the possibility of improving our circumstances, or our community, or the world at large. It is useful to consider that we have the potential to influence our colleagues and leaders in their livelihood pursuits, and perhaps help mindfully guide the unfolding impermanence in the direction of delivering increasing value. We can also influence change as we spend mindfully. As we purchase products and services, we support and encourage organizations to adjust their value propositions and delivery processes. In a manner, we are instructing them about the sorts of changes we welcome and those that we do not. As we pay our taxes mindfully, and lawfully, we should be reminded that we are right to expect value from government as well. If dissatisfied, we have means available to communicate and advocate for improvement. It may be useful to remind elected officials of the impermanence of their roles from time to time. Similarly, charities and not-for-profits can be influenced to increase efficiencies and accountabilities, and tasked to demonstrate results. Even if they do not, we have the power to create our own.

Perhaps of the greatest significance to me is the relationship between change and our opportunities to invest, and create wealth. As entrepreneurs identify and formulate solutions to problems arising from change, they may require investment capital to develop, grow, and scale processes for value delivery. Those who execute well have the potential to receive significant reward for the needs they satisfy and happiness they create. Investors participating in primary market securities can benefit from the impermanence that stimulates these ventures. Even fluctuations in secondary investment markets, like those of 2008 and 2009, create very significant opportunities for investors to buy low and sell high. Change makes this possible. As we achieve our financial goals, from value delivery to mindful investing, we may realize a degree of wealth that eliminates the need for other forms of livelihood. Our Right Livelihood may literally derive from our mindful investing.

The purveyor of these investment products, and the associated promises of financial success – the financial services industry – has itself between affected by many significant changes over recent years. Advancements in information management and communications, which have impacted almost every facet of modern life, have been particularly disruptive to those providing financial products and services. For every instance where technology improves, and comes to perform an activity that used to be performed by a human, a person is no longer completing that task. At first, such developments were welcomed. When I started my very first full-time job in 1987 after graduating from university, as a stock broker's assistant, computers had just been introduced to the office. The one I had nearly filled my desk, and provided me with some information about the market (the bid, the ask, trade volumes, etc.) of some publicly traded securities. I did not feel threatened by its presence, and most of the work still required the efforts of a person. Yet, I have witnessed how, from these humble beginnings, technology slowly comes to provide ever-increasing degrees of value to increasing numbers of people. The implication is that financial representatives are challenged themselves to be able to be the providers of that value. The less value that a person provides, the less opportunity they have for financial reward. Indeed, I have noticed an increase in announcements from larger financial institutions about plans to reduce their workforce and reallocate resources to additional technological developments.

In some instances, these developments in the financial services industry have not yet led to improved value propositions for consumers. Rather, the response from some participants is to attempt to halt or at least slow the changes, in an effort to retain the business models that suit their interests. Yet, others embrace these changes and relish the challenges that come. They see an opportunity to adjust and improve their value propositions, and to communicate their evolving value to the market. Wisely, they accept

## Impermanence and Opportunity

impermanence, not as a threat, but as a necessary precondition to provide new forms of value with new delivery processes. In my mind, the victor in the battle between old and new business models will be determined by consumer perceptions of trustworthiness.

I believe that value delivery processes featuring the increasing use of technology (over traditional human models) are seeking, and will continue to seek, acceptance from the market by communicating superior trustworthiness relative to their competitors. Moreover, I see this phenomenon as being especially prevalent in the financial services industry. An upstart technology-based delivery system, for example, could attempt to communicate that it is more worthy of ability trust: it might propose to the market that this system is more able to provide value, or is able to provide a superior value. It might hold out as evidence in support of this claim that, as it is a technology-based system, it can provide more information, that is more accurate and more current, and is delivered faster and more conveniently. It can be expected to propose that these improvements lead to better-informed decision-making and outcomes for the consumer. It may even be able to offer an increased value at a lower price. Further, such a disrupting upstart would communicate that it is more worthy of integrity trust. It might suggest to consumers that, by reducing the role of humans, it is increasing the likelihood that the value that can be provided actually will be provided. It might propose, for example, that humans are influenced by specific reward and recognition systems, and may be unable to put the needs of the consumer ahead of their own needs. Such influences, they may argue, are eliminated or significantly reduced, by their new and improved value delivery system, resulting in a greater likelihood of increased happiness.

Thankfully, there is at least one notable facet of the investment management sector of the financial services industry that is successfully combining human value delivery with technological innovations for increasing consumer benefit. That sector is referred to as portfolio management.

A Portfolio Manager selects and purchases a variety of securities for the investors. However, these Portfolio Managers may have much greater flexibility in terms of the securities they select, and the strategies they can implement, when compared to traditional investment funds. Further, they can manage these portfolios with discretion: that is, without having to seek permission from each investor. This permits these managers to buy and sell quickly, taking advantage of opportunities as they are presented. Many Portfolio Managers offer these portfolios as a pool or pools of securities. Individual investors participate in the pool. When securities are purchased and sold, each investor in the pool benefits at the same time, regardless of how much money they have invested, or how close they are to the Portfolio Managers. This form of management provides for a fair and even distribution of the value proposition to the market.

Historically, this form of invest management may have been unavailable to most investors. Minimum household account sizes were higher than most could afford – even $1 million or more. Yet, with the use of technology, such services have become available to regular investors, with ever decreasing household minimums – in some cases, as low as a few hundred or a few thousand dollars. Additionally, technology is providing new client engagement and communications processes that are creative, innovative, and convenient, resulting in easier access to the services. Technology is also enabling the delivery processes to provide this attractive value position for lower costs than many traditional investment funds. This downward pressure on prices is being experienced as a reduction in revenue for those purveyors of traditional investments and with traditional business models. As such, some of the participants in the financial services industry are struggling to communicate their relative value proposition to consumers in the wake of these changes.

This form of technology-supported, Portfolio Manager, pooled investment, value delivery process ranks as among the most trustworthy of value propositions available to investors. By accessing

## Impermanence and Opportunity

a wider range of investments, using a wider range of strategies, and with cost-improving efficiencies, many contemporary Portfolio Managers are better able to deliver on the promise of value. They are more worthy of the ability trust, and consumers are more likely to achieve their investment objectives and financial goals. Further, as Portfolio Managers have discretionary ability, they are held to the highest legal standard of care for their clients. In other words, they have a fiduciary duty to consumers to consider their needs and wants first. (This is a far cry from the suitability obligation standard to which most financial representatives are subject.) Since Portfolio Managers can manage investment proceeds in a pool, and select and trade securities for all participants simultaneously, it is most likely that each investor will receive the value that others receive. It is unlikely that they will be left out of the value delivery processes. However, this discretionary power could be misused by unscrupulous and persuasive swindlers, resulting in the potential for great harm to consumers. As such, it is a category of registration that is now managed very closely by securities regulators, and is quite difficult to achieve. It tends to require more experience, and more advanced education and designations, than other registration categories. These designations often come with a requirement for the financial representative to adhere to strict codes of professional ethics. Additional protective measures for consumers also include the requirement that a Portfolio Manager retain the services of an independent trustee and custodian to affirm that processes are indeed being managed as reported. For these reasons, the value delivery processes of registered Portfolio Managers can now be considered as among the most worthy of integrity trust.

In my experience, those who aspire to be Portfolio Managers tend to be driven by strong values. They believe that the work they do is important, as it can contribute significantly to the financial success of their clients. Moreover, they tend to be motivated by the idea that the best investment strategies should be available to all, regardless of the amount of money they have to invest. Some are vocal advocates in support of transparency for consumers, and even strive to have the cost of investment management reduced! The strength of these values may also be expressed in the specific investments selected. For example, some will provide additional value to clients by including socially responsible, environmental, or impact investment strategies.

Through all aspects of livelihood, and in the many ways we spend and invest the rewards of our livelihood, impermanence is the creator of opportunity. We can benefit personally from this, and we can be part of the processes that help others benefit. Change is the reason that new forms of value can be provided, and it helps make possible the financial reward that can follow. For those seeking financial success and wealth, change should therefore be pursued and embraced. Moreover, through our actions and our communications, we can influence the direction of these changes. We can guide the providers of products and services, and especially those in the financial services industry, toward the sorts of value we are seeking. This is our responsibility, and it is critical if those providers are to increase our happiness and reduce our suffering. We play an important role in their pursuit of Right Livelihood. As such, we must be ready for the change and so we must be prepared to forgo attachments. Especially, we must be prepared to let go of ideas and perspectives that are not providing us with what we need to go forward. We must allow ourselves to not be limited by a specific past or a specific present, as if those will necessitate any specific future. By letting go, we are preparing ourselves to attain.

There is a wonderful, Buddhist-inspired parable that highlights the limiting nature of attachments.

Four friends were walking together along a great lake. They were complaining about their struggles and difficulties. They were complaining about the general unhappiness of their village, where they each had spent their entire life. They had heard about a beautiful village on the other shore, on the other side of the lake. It was said that, in that village, all could lead happy, fulfilled lives, helping

## Impermanence and Opportunity

others and being helped in return. Alas, the friends could not swim across the lake, as it was too wide and too deep. So, they would walk along the shore and gaze across the lake, trying to imagine what their life might be like in the other village.

One day the four friends came along four unknown objects on the shore. They were four boats. The friends had never seen a boat before. The boats were being attended to by an elder of the village. The wise elder explained that the boats could be used to travel the long distance across the lake, and invited the friends to embark.

One friend was disturbed by the idea of leaving. Even though that friend was unhappy in the village, that friend could not enter the boat. The attachment to the present was more comforting than the prospect of going towards the unknown. The friend stayed and did not realize the promise of happiness.

The other friends each entered a boat, and began the long journey across the lake. The friends survived sun and storm, hunger and thirst, and, with much effort, eventually learned how to navigate their boat. Each friend managed to reach the other shore.

One friend was grateful for the boat, and attached to the experience of the journey. So much so, that the friend remained with the boat, and did not proceed along the path from the lake to the village, and the promise of happiness.

Another friend was also attached to the boat, to such a great degree that the friend dragged and carried the boat along the path, never letting it go. That friend was so burdened by the boat, that the promise of happiness was not realized.

The final friend was grateful for the boat and the experience. That friend knew though, that the boat had served its purpose. That friend pushed the boat from the shore, in the direction of the elder waiting on the other side. That friend continued on the path, entered the village, unattached, and was ready to pursue the promise of happiness.

# 11
# A Path Forward

An intellectual journey can be like a physical journey. We often begin from a place of comfort and familiarity. This may be a place of ideas, perspectives, values and influences. From here we set a course. We may not have a clear sense of where we are going, but perhaps we have some form of compass as a guide. In the case of the journey that I have attempted to describe, the guide can be thought of as a moral compass. Some may feel such a journey would require a choice of direction: if we follow one path, we might find financial success and wealth; if we take the path in the opposite direction, we might find that we will behave morally and help others. I am suggesting that the moral compass of a Buddhist can have each of us arrive in both destinations simultaneously. It can be one path forward.

Moreover, along this path, I have invited readers to pause to appreciate what I consider to be more significant points of interest. Here is a summary:

> The Wealthy Buddhist seeks understanding with an open mind – a beginner's mind. We should seek opinions and ideas beyond those that are presented to us by our family, our community, our school, or our religion. Wealth is more likely to result from seeking, and being open to, new sources of information and perspectives.

> The Wealthy Buddhist recognizes that people are often unhappy, even to the point of suffering, and acknowledges that

our livelihood behaviour can be a considerable cause. We should aspire to Right Livelihood, and seek to reduce suffering and increase happiness through our livelihood pursuits.

The Wealthy Buddhist understands success as the result of helping others successfully gain value. We should understand financial reward can be a measurement of the amount and quality of value provided. Wealth can result from providing an unusual amount value, resulting in the increased happiness and reduced suffering for an unusual number of people.

The Wealthy Buddhist sees problems and unhappiness, wants and needs, as an opportunity. With an entrepreneurial spirit, we should look for solutions to these problems, and participate in processes that delivery value.

The Wealthy Buddhist recognizes that successful value delivery processes grow, and come to include a complex array of stakeholders. Regardless of our role in these processes, we should act as a leader in the encouragement of the reduction of harm, and the increase of happiness, on balance, to all stakeholders.

The Wealthy Buddhist will focus on developing skills and strategies to communicate that value can and will be delivered. We should ensure that we are worthy of ability trust and integrity trust, and ensure that we can communicate that to stakeholders.

The Wealthy Buddhist spends to receive value, and to provide others with the opportunity provide value. We should spend mindfully – influencing providers of products and services, government agencies, and not-for-profits to engage in Right Livelihood.

### A Path Forward

The Wealthy Buddhist invests to enable value delivery process, and receive commensurate reward. We should invest mindfully – influencing organizations to increase happiness and reduce suffering.

The Wealthy Buddhist expects value from the financial services industry and its representatives. We must expect a clear value proposition, and evidence to confirm ability trust and integrity trust.

The Wealthy Buddhist forgoes attachment, and accepts impermanence as a catalyst for the opportunity to receive and provide value. We must accept that change supports the pursuit of Right Livelihood. We must be ready to let go of that which is no longer providing value, and seek new opportunities to increase happiness.

The success of this journey might be measured by the usefulness of the ideas explored along the way. If you feel you are better enabled to do well for yourself, and do good for others, I hope you would, therefore, measure this journey as worthwhile. If you are now better able to make choices, or understand choices you have already made, then my efforts may be understood as providing some value.

As I reflect on some of my own choices, I see instances of success and instances of failure. I see times and circumstances when I might have made other choices, and others when I am comfortable with the choices I made. When I consider the moral appropriateness of running to return the lottery ticket, for example, I am comfortable that I was engaging in Right Livelihood. I had my role in the value delivery processes of the store where I worked, contributing to potential for increased happiness of the customers. The distribution of lottery tickets was overseen by government, and, at that time, proceeds were typically used to help fund not-for-profit organizations. Ironically, I understand that the amateur football association for which my disappointed father volunteered was also a beneficiary. As such, I was helping the customer to spend mindfully. However, he was not so mindful as to see that he actually had a winning ticket. I was able to bring this to his awareness, thereby completing the delivery of value. I do not know whether or not he was able to turn those winnings into further value delivery, and happiness for himself or others. However, out of those winnings, he gifted me with $200. I used that money to invest in further education, and the pursuit of success.

# About the Author

Rod Burylo has been writing and speaking on the topic of ethics and wealth for over 30 years. His unique perspectives are the result of an unusual background: as a philosopher, as an award-winning financial advisor, as a Buddhist leader, as a financial services executive, and as a consultant to entrepreneurs.

During his undergraduate and post baccalaureate studies at University of Calgary and Simon Fraser University, he focused on jurisprudence and applied ethics, including research in medical ethics. Upon graduation, he entered the financial services industry as a stock broker's assistant, and became a columnist – writing on the topic of business and financial ethics.

Burylo's career has taken him through every major sector of the financial services industry, and in a wide variety of roles, from front-line, retail sales, to branch management, to Chief Compliance Officer and Director. This included personal banking and lending roles with Royal Bank, as well as financial planning (with insurance and mutual fund advisory) for Investors Group and Great West Life. Along the way, he earned numerous licenses and registrations, including Certified Financial Planner (CFP®) designation.

With a passion for teaching, he was invited to begin to train and mentor other financial advisors, and soon became an Associate Regional Director for one of Investors Group's most successful branches. During this time, he wrote his first book, *Awesome Client Events*, and began to train professionals throughout North America.

Burylo co-founded Canadian's Retiring Abroad, a financial advisory business focused on international retirement planning, and became a recipient of a coveted Advisor of the Year Award. This work lead to international speaking engagements, and additional writing as a columnist, and media contributor and expert source.

Burylo became increasingly active in the Buddhist community, and spent many years as a Director of the Calgary Buddhist Temple, including roles as Vice President and President. He Chaired the Capital Committee, responsible for fundraising towards a significant renovation of the temple, and developed a community communications strategy. He provided strategic support and education to Buddhist leaders in Canada and the United States, and was invited to speak on the topic of Right Livelihood at a World Buddhist Conference.

Professionally, Burylo went on to establish one of Canada's first Exempt Market Dealerships, which became part of Canada's largest and best-known private equity dealerships. He served as Chief Compliance Officer and Director before exiting in 2012. During this time, his second book, *More Awesome Client Events* was published.

Since that time, he has been providing consulting and board support to a variety of different organizations, including exempt market dealerships, investment fund managers, and portfolio managers. He completed his Chartered Investment Manager (CIM®) designation, and is a recipient of the prestigious Fellow of the Canadian Securities Institute (FCSI®) designation. He served as Director for National Exempt Market Association, where he drafted the association's code of ethics.

Today, Rod Burylo is an Associate Portfolio Manager and Business Development Manager for Croft Financial Group. He serves on the board of a public company, and is a board advisor and consultant for private companies in the finance, investment and accounting sectors. He is a Director and Board Chair for the Foundation for the Advancement of Entrepreneurship. He designs and delivers ethics and professional responsibility classes for financial advisors, and provides lectures on the topic of trust, communications, and technology.

www.ingramcontent.com/pod-product-compliance
Lightning Source LLC
Chambersburg PA
CBHW030141170426
43199CB00008B/153